3/07

The Book of David

David Steinberg

Simon & Schuster

New York   London   Toronto   Sydney

SIMON & SCHUSTER
Rockefeller Center
1230 Avenue of the Americas
New York, NY 10020

SIMON & SCHUSTER and colophon are registered trademarks of
Simon & Schuster, Inc.

For information about special discounts for bulk purchases,
please contact Simon & Schuster Special Sales at
1-800-456-6798 or business@simonandschuster.com

Designed by Nancy Singer Olaguera

Manufactured in the United States of America

1   3   5   7   9   10   8   6   4   2

Library of Congress Cataloging-in-Publication Data

Steinberg, David.
The book of David / David Steinberg.
p.   cm.
1. Steinberg, David.
2. Comedians—Canada—Biography I. Title
PN2308S73A3 2007
792.702'8'92—dc22   2007007697
ISBN-13: 978–0–7432–7232–2
ISBN-10: 0–7432–7232–3

ACKNOWLEDGMENTS

I'd first like to thank my collaborator, Joel Engel, who collaborated with me so well when we were collaborating.

I'd also like to thank my editor, David Rosenthal, for laughing at all the right parts and then making me laugh at all the wrong parts.

To my wife, Robyn.

To Tammy and Harry.

And to the memory of my beloved brother, Fishy.

The Book
of David

AUTHOR'S APOLOGIA

The Bible is the direct word of God. Or it's not. We don't really know, do we?

Yes, people of faith have faith that it is. But even they have to agree that the words themselves, even if divinely inspired, were not exactly committed to paper (or stone) by God. For though He is omnipotent, omniscient, and possibly omnipresent, He apparently has poor handwriting. Which means that these words we've loved and studied and lived by for thousands of years were inscribed by the hands of men. Human men. Which should immediately make the project a little suspect in the literalness department.

After all, such men as these who long ago bothered to take the time and effort to record the words for posterity without the benefit of word processing and tape recorders are the same type of men who enjoy telling stories. I've met a few of them in my day, and the one thing I can say for sure about such men is that they cannot be trusted to take dictation. Their natural instinct is to add a little twist here and there—you know, tweak the narrative to make it sexier, more violent, more preachy; more anything, actually, as long as it ends up more interesting and therefore memorable.

Hey, you think your favorite joke was born intact out of the womb? Long before you first heard it, that masterpiece of setup and surprise had been told and retold hundreds of times by people who'd each change a little detail on the fly in order to get a bigger laugh, eventually resulting in the joke you love. And where did they get that inclination to edit and create? From God, of course, in whose image we're all made. So it's not such a stretch to imagine Him looking over the shoulder of His scribes as they played a biblical game of Telephone, compressing a little history or exaggerating the facts, and thinking to Himself, *Hmmm, that's not quite the way I meant it, but it's pretty good.*

If indeed the Almighty, blessed be He, intended us to retell these stories throughout eternity, He would've wanted them to be as strong as possible. Otherwise, as His beloved Darwin pointed out, they wouldn't stand a chance of surviving. Which means that when the legend becomes fact, you gotta go with the *National Enquirer*'s version. So saith the Lord. And if He didn't, He should have.

David Steinberg
June 2007

THE OLD TESTAMENT

1

In the beginning—well, maybe it wasn't exactly the beginning. It could have been closer to the middle, or, depending on what happens in the Mideast, nearer the end than anyone would care to think about, which is how de Nile got its name. But it was sometime after that pleasant Sunday during the Big Bang years when the Eternal One, blessed be He and His name which you are not allowed to utter aloud or even spell out completely, had taken the formless, black, cold earth and exhaled holy carbon dioxide into its lungs (technically not CPR, because earth wasn't yet alive), declaring that there would be light—but not just any light; it should be a particular light, not too bright yet good for reading. And God called this light "day," though of course it is not called day in every language. In Szechuan, for example, the word for day is not pronounceable by nonnative speakers, but since only heathen unbelievers (will *they* be sorry) live in China,

God chose to call the light by its verbal symbol in English, which until recently was the main language of the formerly God-fearing United States. (See: Day of Reckoning.)

Then did God declare that there should be a firmament in the midst of the waters, as if He had a choice unless He wanted His peoples to be fishes (but let's not skip ahead). Forsooth, you should know that He did indeed consider such a state for a while before deciding against it on the grounds that He needed a drier place to live. Thus, on the second morning He gatherest up the waters together in one place, so He could keep an eye on things when He eventually commanded man to evolve and crawl out of the primordial ooze onto dry land; for that to happen, of course, He had to actually have dry land. *Capisce?* He called the dry land Earth, this time with a capital E, in order to confuse writers and students and Green Party functionaries with the difference between Earth and earth—as in He and Him and His inscrutable sense of humor. Lo (and behold), on the Earth, God discovered that He had a Green Thumb. You want to talk creativity? Stuff grew everywhere, some of it poisonous, but no matter. He pronounced it good, because He does not have self-esteem issues, even though His own backstory is a little vague (*How did I get all this power?*).

Now cameth the third morning. He was groggy, for He had stayed up all night fretting and thinking about what to do next—waiting, if you must know, for inspiration. Oh then did His voice thunder onto the landscape, which was already overgrown and in need of pruning: "Let there be lights in the firmament of the heavens to separate the day from the night; and let them be for signs and for seasons and for days and years, and let them be lights in the firmament of the heavens to give light upon the earth."

All of which is to say merely that He created the sun and moon and stars (He was not, at first, a God of few words). And that was pretty good, too, or at least He thought so until He realized how all that good light was going to waste—and trees were falling in the forests without Immanuel Kant hearing them.

Thus, on the fourth day He filled the air with bugs and birds, and the oceans with some good Northern whitefish but also a lot of *traife*, and He commanded them to multiply, and they listened and they obeyed, especially the bugs, so that now it's so bad some days in Miami, you could be forgiven for spraying a few of God's creatures that have been just a little too fruitful. Understand ye that, at the time He animated all of His creatures, God wasn't really into considering the consequences of His actions or focus-grouping them, for He was too involved in His many works, thinking how He really had it going now. And that explains the context in which He created beasts and other violent things to run around killing and eating each other.

For some reason, He thought that that was good, too. (He has never acknowledged that the law of the jungle may have been a mistake, not even when Rousseau came up with a better idea. Except for some Freudian guilt over the casualty toll from an early flood, He obstinately insists that first drafts are for sissies and lesser gods.)

But then did something begin to gnaw at Him, and it was not one of His beasts; He sensed a vital piece missing from the master plan. Hallelujah, yes: Man! He would create man, and—once again evincing that mischievous ear for language—man would be both man and woman. *That should hold them for a while,* He thought. And yet, His emptiness persisted—an incredibly big emptiness. *What is that missing link?* He wondered as His anthropomorphic fingers stroked His untouchable chin, feeling the pressure to create something big and new and yet coming up empty, for He could not manage to think outside the box. Thus did He ponder whether God can create an image that He cannot live up to.

And then after a good night's sleep He slapped his forehead and remembered what He had chosen to forget: Yes, He would invent free will and implant it into man so that man could disobey Him—and in that way the real fun of being God and having a front-row seat at billions of small Greek tragedies over countless millennia could begin in earnest. It was sublime. It was transcendent. It was foolproof. It would be a living hell.

But wait, for in an inspired coda God decided to create man in His own image.

"Now *that's* good," He pronounced, clapping His unknowable hands in joy—and inadvertently causing a thunderstorm that wiped out sixty-one species, including a plant that would've one day cured cancer, which He had also invented on the assumption that man would enjoy the discovery process.

But what now had He wrought? Winners and losers. God, you see, is a master of disguise. Brad Pitt and Rasputin? Both are made in His image. Angelina Jolie and Phyllis Schlafly? Yea, they too.

And so, chaos began to reign, which meant that God's work was at last done. It had taken six days, and He was quite naturally exhausted. On the seventh day He slept in—right through dinner. Some say He's been asleep ever since, but some are going to have a nasty surprise waiting for them on the other side.

Anyway, when the time was right, He created the Steinbergs.

Poor God.

2

And so it did come to pass in the way that such matters often come to pass in this world banished from Eden because of an apple tasted by someone whose curiosity had been instilled by a Creator who then punished the curious and all their progeny for the same curiosity, that the sons of the sons of the sons of Steinberg with their chosen mates did run from the Cossacks on horses who enjoyed to use their heads for polo. Such was daily life for the Steinbergs and their kind of people in Siberia adjacent, under a ruler who cared not for their excellence in the grocery business and in general did not show them adequate appreciation.

Cruel taskmasters dealt with them harshly; it was a harsh life. And shrewdly did the Steinbergs plot their escape to another dominion, doing so without the benefit of travel brochures or Expedia.com. But *shrewdly* is not the same as *well*. Compared to the frigid, barren new land, the old land looked like Boca in June. They called the name of this new land Winnipeg, which is Yiddish for something that is funny only in Yiddish.

Thus did Winnipeg become overrun with Steinbergs and with their kind of people. Into two groups did such people split. The first group was Communists. The second group was people other than Communists. God did not seem all that excited about either group.

3

Yascha Steinberg had hoped to make his troth but he did not know what troth meant or how a troth got made, so he wed Ruth Runya, who had the same cherry lips as her mother but without the stem. He promised her land, and she was well pleased with the promise and in the meantime insisted on a new winter coat, which he gave her, and then she wished aloud for some modest piece of jewelry that she might call her own, which he gave her (on a grocer's earnings!), and then for a car, which he also gave—and she was now of course better pleased. Her womb was quickly blessed, a boy and then a girl and then another boy, and for Ruth this was blessing enough. From now on let another woman be so blessed, she declared, warning Yascha that he must make an early exodus on those nights of connubial recreation; she had, she insisted, all the blessings any non-Catholic woman could bear, and any more blessings would not be a blessing.

Yascha did not know whether he himself could endure another blessing—maybe he could, maybe he couldn't—but he had been a rabbi before he sold cottage cheese and artichoke hearts, and in his Talmudic wisdom he sensed that another blessing on his wife would lessen her marital effectiveness. That is why he made certain to heed her warning. And he did so diligently and carefully for ten years, and except for the fact that he had so far failed to deliver on the land that he had promised (these were good years for groceries but not good enough to buy land at such inflated prices), all was well in the house of Steinberg as long as you did not drive with Yascha, who believed that the rearview mirror hung where it did in order that he may adjust his hat properly before arriving at his destination.

Then came Purim, the festival celebrating capital punishment for which God commands obscene drunkenness, and in his dizzy peppermint-schnapps passion Yascha forgot the early exodus decree, just this once, and did not make his exit before the Red Sea closed up. When his wife saw what he had done, she attempted to smite him.

"You putz," she cried.

And so it came to pass as it sometimes does, God misunderstood her cry of disgust for ecstasy, and blessed her with child.

And the child was named David, which in Hebrew means "a punishment from God."*

"So much," Ruth said, "for the promised land."

---

* The name David does not really mean "punishment from God," but that is what I was led to believe for my first thirty years. Imagine my surprise—and therapy bills—when I discovered that it means "beloved one."

4

The child David did not like the truth. He did not like rules. He did not like school. He liked movies after school and did not like that his life was not filled with singing and dancing in the rain like *Singing in the Rain*.* Ruth and Yascha did not understand any of this about their fourth child until their knowledge was increased to an awareness that school did not, in fact, begin at noon and end at five. Their hearts were hardened and they dealt severely with David and they commanded him to cease his movie adventures. David said, "You are not God."

---

* The first movie I ever saw was *The Jolson Story*, which immediately inspired me to impersonate the great singer. My family quickly got tired of seeing me, in blackface, down on one knee, mouth open like a vacuole, performing at Passover Seders. Nor did my mother enjoy being called "Mammy."

But Yascha's heart was not moved by his delightful child on whom he spared the rod (for he was not as fast a runner as David). He had learned the meaning of the English words "juvenile delinquent" and they were much on his mind when he said to Ruth, "I'm afraid he'll try to send frogs and gnats."

Indeed, David now wandered the afternoon streets of Winnipeg, adrift in mental lies, and thus did catastrophe and plagues now descend upon the city—fires, mayhem, children speaking in blue tongues, lactose intolerance. Everywhere that David wandered disasters occurred in his wake—nothing that could be pinned on David directly, but still the citizens were concerned with the coincidences which they referred to as circumstantial evidence. A committee of them knocked on the Steinbergs' door and were disappointed to hear from David that Yascha and Ruth had recently returned to Russia, abandoning their children for the joys of the motherland. These were the proverbial "some of the people" whom you can fool all of the time, but soon there arrived at the door a second group that would not be fooled a second time, and when Yascha and Ruth read the presentation of proof they wept and wailed and rent their garments as would the parents of a child upon learning that he is the antichrist. And they of course offered David money for movies after school, as many movies as he wanted. Said Yascha, "At least that way there'll be two hours when he won't burn down the neighborhood."

So now David watched movies in the afternoon, and Winnipeg was saved from a kind of wrath that no one could explain without violating the commandment not to take the Lord's name in vain. Only one time did David steal—a small gold maple leaf from Hudson Bay Department Store.* The detective who seized him soon beat his breast and wailed with sympathy to hear that David's parents had returned to Russia without him, and David was conveyed home in a police cruiser while eating a triple scoop of chocolate chip.

---

* The thief was actually Alvin Brownstein, who pinned the crime on me before becoming a famous and successful lawyer. Who knows what secret crimes he's gotten away with since then.

5

od had been watching David cause his friends to laugh by the telling of lies. They were humorous lies, He inferred; and David's friends enjoyed them, He saw. And so God felt envious of their mirth, for it looked like good mirth. He checked His commandments and noted the description of Him as "jealous," then confirmed that "Thou Shalt Not Lie" had not made the final cut of His prohibitions—unless, of course, the lying concerns neighbors, whose ass they were not allowed to covet (though a good spanking properly administered under the right circumstances with the right neighbor was not necessarily a bad thing).

But these of His multitudes were not neighbors of David, and they all derived from the male of the species. So David did not covet their asses (not that there's anything wrong with it), which therefore made the laughter acceptable entertainment. And God wanted in on it, not having laughed deeply since William Shatner covered "Lucy in the Sky with Diamonds."

Of course, being the Lord God Almighty, He had several options open to Him, and this time, just for a change, He settled on speaking directly to David, who was alone on the basketball court, practicing his crossover dribble. Thinking back, He realized that He had not spoken directly to one of His multitudes since Dylan found Him and He had to pretend to be someone else. Nonetheless, His booming voice sounded surprisingly gentle, considering.

"David," He said, "it's God. Over here."

David recognized that this was God calling, but he ignored Him for the same reason that he ignored his parents—because there were better things to do. Like practice the Cousy no-look pass.*

God did not mind His chops busted. He was used to His people blowing Him off whenever it was more convenient for them. And indeed, David's defiance gave His quick and creative mind an idea for an elaborate plan of great mystery. Which is always the best that can be said of His plans.

Again, God spoke to David. He said, "Hey!"

And again David ignored God, so again God spoke to David. He said, "David, listen to Me. I've got an opening for a good man in the Northern Territories. You interested?"

---

* I'm not certain that the first time God spoke to me occurred while I was playing basketball. But given that I hadn't yet discovered two other popular Winnipeg pastimes of the 1950s—masturbation and dry humping—it might very well have been during hoops.

An opening in the Northern Territories? David heard the offer but it was without appeal and so he did not ponder, and because he did not ponder he did not respond. He continued ignoring God while gaily practicing his jump shot—and scheming to convince that red-gold goddess Esther Rambam to bear the grandeur of her lush gold bosom to him. Strictly speaking, she was not his neighbor, as she lived eight blocks over and two down; therefore, coveting her ass was uncommanded against.

In his deceitful deafness, David was not being coy with God the way he wished Esther Rambam would be coy with him. Just as a gag, he considered doing his dead-on "You talkin' to me" De Niro. But he had studied God and His mysterious ways in school, and had deduced that when it came to cherished human contact, God experienced intimacy issues. Which was a conclusion that had once incited bedlam in his Nearer My God to Thee 101 section.

Anyway, David could see no direct benefit in attempting to close the distance between him and a Being who had taken four hundred years before figuring out how to get His chosen people out of slavery—and then hadn't even allowed them time enough to bake a little bread and maybe some hamantaschen for the trip. What, would an extra half hour have killed Him? Instead of hurry up and wait, this was suffer and hurry up. The whole episode seemed to David a little on the passive-aggressive side, and he said that if you looked objectively at the facts of His life, God was exactly the kind of "element" your mother was always warning you to stay away from, like those horrible Rosenthals over on Saskatchewan Avenue.

All things considered, David was unmoved by His

laws of physics and His great cosmic game of craps, and he thought God had made a stunning tactical error by demanding that His subjects hold feasts to Him and celebrate the mysteriousness of His ways so often in at least four major religions.

And what could be said about God's apparent need for people to believe in Him while at the same time pretending not to exist? To David, it bordered on the psychotic. David sensed that it would've been better if God allowed you to throw Him an occasional surprise party or something, though of course there was no way to surprise God, since He already knew everything you were planning, just like the children in *Village of the Damned* who could read behind the brick wall in George Sanders's mind that was supposed to be hiding dynamite in the briefcase.

So maybe that was why God demanded so many holidays, and maybe that was why God appeared so mysterious: He was lonely. Hell, what God wouldn't be under those circumstances? Even so, David did not feel up to going out and having a few brewskis with the Supreme Being. Why should he? This was God Almighty; obviously, He'd known what the gig was about when He took it. And besides, He had made the rules, and He was in a position to change them, if He wanted.

So no, David did not suffer the yearning for a personal relationship with God, like that smarmy kreplach-polisher Schlomo Mutsche, who didn't realize that God never calls on the guy with his hand raised.

But what about this opening in the Northern Territories that God had mentioned? David did have to admit that it was more than a little flattering to have the Creator

Himself refuse to take no for an answer, for David did feel curious about a few things and would have liked to ask some questions:

Why, for example, if Abraham had had the *cojones* to try to argue God out of torching Sodom and Gomorrah, did he soon turn into a good Nazi by binding his own son for slaughter on command?

And why didn't the great Noah try talking God out of drowning everyone? Shouldn't he have suggested Plan B—that the Almighty start with one of the minor countries (say, France) as a warning shot?

Or was it that God had been inspired to do the full-on flood thing after reading Gilgamesh in the original Babylonian?

Oh, and what had Mrs. Noah said to Noah after the waters receded, when he broke it to her that they'd been tasked with repopulating the world? "Get that thing out of here"?

All these things and more David was curious about—just not curious enough to stop practicing his between-the-legs dribble and engage God in conversation.

Undeterred, God continued to hound David—not like a stalker, exactly, but it was annoying nonetheless.

And at last David gave in and returned God's call.

David said, "All right, God, make your best case. You got one minute."

God said, "David, don't you know that there is more to life than basketball and girls? Be realistic."

"Realistic?" uttered David. "Be realistic?! A voice comes out of nowhere and claims He created the world in six days, but we can't see you, we're just supposed to believe in you on faith alone, and *I'm* the one who's gotta be realistic?"

"Good point," said God. "But if I show you to Me, then you will not need faith; you will have proof. And then, what's the point of faith?"

Hmm. For a moment, David was somewhat moved by God's use of the semicolon. But then he realized that the tautology was even less impressive than Descartes's narcissistic idiocy about thinking ergo being. This disappointment caused David to refuse speaking with capitalized pronouns. He said, "Listen, God, I don't know if you know this—I mean, you should—but Winnipeg is the Missouri of the North. You're gonna have to show yourself if you want me on your team."

Frankly, David cared not one way or another whether God existed. What was the big deal about whether God existed? In the words of his uncle Schmuel, "Exist, not exist—we're stuck here." Exactly.

"That's not possible," said God.

"Oh, yeah?" said David.

He decided to call God's bluff, which he knew from his studies to be an ancient and honorable tradition among Jews—as when Jacob slapped a hammerlock on an angel and instead of being snuffed out got the cute nickname "Israel," which translates to "You have taken God two out of three falls."

Thus did David declare, "I have faith now, God. I have faith that when I light my house on fire, it will not be consumed."

David raised his father's bottle of peppermint schnapps with a sweaty basketball sock in the lip and struck a match to ignite a Molotov cocktail. He had free will, and could torch the place if he so chose. But would he so choose?

God called upon His foresight vision, which He both-
ers to use only sometimes in order to see what someone
is going to do with his free will before he does it, and He
foresaw that David was hoping for God to stop him but did
not trust God to intercede on behalf of the house and fur-
nishings. Such ruminations put God in the catbird seat.

Perhaps, thought David, *this will become one of His impla-
cably mysterious fiascos, like the Crusades and Pat Buchanan.
Perhaps God will let the house burn down and I'll go to prison
for arson, and in prison I will cry out, "Oh, God, I believe, I
believe. Hear my prayers," but by then my faith will come too
late to stop half of Manitoba's skinheads from making me their
bitch.*

David blew out the match.

"All right, God, you win," he said. "Dammit."

But God did not gloat over his victory, for the night
was young. He said, "David, you believe in the magnifi-
cence of Esther Rambam's nakedness, don't you?"

"Yes, of course, God."

"But you've not seen that, either."

David started to say, "Good point," knowing that the
one God, if this were He, had many times witnessed the
glory of David's manhood fill the bedroom when David
was alone with his sexual thoughts, which had the tactile
palpability of creamy twin mounds topped by rose-hard-
ened tips.

But instead David said, "God, that's so 1st century B.C.
It just makes me doubt you even more, that you would stoop
so low—like that burning bush stunt. Why a burning bush?
Why not a talking tree, or a flying squirrel, or, for that matter,
why not a text message? And how about the ten plagues and

the Egyptians? The way you did it, you come off like some dime-store magician. Don't you realize that? And do you really, honestly, truly expect us to believe you dictated the five books to Moses? With chisel on stone? Come on, think about it: An aleph—a single aleph—probably takes half an hour."

God did not answer. He just listened, for He had given man skepticism in the hopes of hearing feedback and sharpening His own skills. Of course, He had also given them the tendency to rubberneck at accidents, thus tying up traffic for hours. And for what?

David continued: "Oh, and how come we're supposed to stone an ox to death for goring someone? What's up with that? You're the one who made the ox a beast, but you want us to punish it for that—and yet it's okay to sell one's daughter? That's just too creepy to take seriously. And what's the big deal about wearing linen and wool together? And why can't we smell our own breath? And horses become glue? How'd that happen?*

"You know, God, I gotta tell you, seems to me you started getting into the cooking sherry around day three or so. And I'm not the only one who thinks that, either. It's no wonder so many people doubt you. So if that's what you want—well, you got it, big fella."

God laughed, just as He'd hoped from David, making a sound that few ever hear—the guffaw of God laughing *with* them. Mostly they hear, if they actually stop to listen and consider such details, the mocking screech of God laughing *at* them, usually when they make plans or sit down to dinner

---

* I also wondered about nocturnal emissions and why there were only five senses.

with their teenage children and expect pleasant conversation. What else does God have to laugh at but such things, given his precognitive perception? Poor God. He can't help anticipating the punch line before you say it, which of course takes the fun out of even the best material.

But now David had made God laugh despite Himself—by insulting Him; go figure—and God was much pleased and much amused, for it helped Him to understand why His multitudes adore Don Rickles. *Yes,* He thought, *they really are made in My image.*

David waited for His laughter to subside before saying to Him, "Hey, if it's comedy you're looking for, go talk to Wayne and Schuster."

God snorted. "Oh, no," He said. "Not Wayne and Schuster."*

"Why not?"

"David, it's you I want. So what about My offer?"

"For a good man in the Northern Territories?" said David.

"Yes."

"Just for the record, Almighty, I noticed You didn't answer any of my questions. But that aside—by a good offer, I assume you mean, point guard in the NBA?"

To which God said, "David, I am a miracle worker, yes, but work with Me, okay? You're five-seven, you're Jewish, you still can't go to your left—and the NBA won't be in Canada till the '90s."

---

* Wayne and Schuster were enormously funny comedy stars on Canadian radio and the subject of serious academic analysis at McGill University. They are known to Americans only as that annoying act on *Ed Sullivan.*

"Really? Not till the '90s? So then I get Esther Ram-bam."

"Of course."

"Great. When?"

"Soon as you marry her."

"Oh, God," David moaned.

To which God retorted, "David, what did you expect, carnal knowledge? It's 1958. The sexual revolution's not for another ten years—twenty in Canada."

"All right, God, I give. What is it you want from me?"

"I want you to say this to the people of Winnipeg. Say, 'I am has sent me to you.'"

Now it was David's turn to laugh, and he took his turn, loud and hearty and derisively, and afterward said, "God, if I say, 'I am has sent me to you,' they'll put me in remedial English."

"Nonsense," He said. "Trust me."

6

avid did not like remedial English. He fled Canada but had inherited his father's relocation skills and so settled in a place where remedial English is the official language—Chicago. Given what had happened, he decided to hide out from God, Whom he did not trust anymore, and so entered the witness protection program for former believers, which is called "university."

At university David met a man who said he could help him. The man said to David, "I am has sent you to me," which rung a bell with David, who noticed that the man thought well of himself—maybe as well of himself as God but without the humility. Still, David listened to the man, who had also fled Canada, because this man Saul Bellow had written books with his own hand, unlike God, who'd needed a ghostwriter.

David read the man's books, and he had notes. He said, "I don't think 'Seize the Night' quite works. Maybe you should go with 'Seize the Day.'* And btw, Carp's a terrible name for a Rain King. How 'bout something a little more white bread—like, uh, Henderson."

The writer Bellow was much amused with David's notes, but only to a point, and soon he became not amused at all.

Then David was amused with the writer Bellow's not being amused, and he remained amused with all things of this world and with how all people (except the writer Bellow and also the writer who was called Philip Roth, to whom David had offered notes on the story "Goodbye, Schenectady") were amused with him. For this was rapidly becoming the leitmotif of his young life, though he had no money and was emptier in the stomach than a dyslexic Hebrew who believes Passover lasts one day but that the fasting of Yom Kippur continues for eight.

At mealtimes, he sought sustenance among gentiles studying the mysterious ways of God, and because David was acquainted personally with His ways, he received car-bohydrates and coffee in exchange for jokes told at God's expense. God was a good sport and did not mind (or if He did, He said nothing), and these future young men of the cloth laughed and lavished praise on David for not being struck dead by lightning and conveyed to hell by demons for his blasphemies—punishments that would certainly

---

* I was pleased to see that Bellow took my suggestion, though his grat-itude for my input and impudence are nowhere on the record—unless you generously count the writer's one and a half times he came to see me at Second City, and his most important novel, *Mr. Steinberg's Planet.*

befall them if they themselves tried getting a laugh out of the crucifixion. One of them offered advice to David on a career that, evidently, only Jews were free to pursue.

He said:

"You should be a comedian."

"What," asked David, "is a comedian?"

7

David had not heard the word *comedian* before, nor had he known that from such a thing one could make a living, God willing. The idea of enjoying capital for appearing on a dais and causing people to laugh and drink was like the baring of a woman's bosom in his mind. Oh, to hear that laughter and count the shekels would be as sweet as making love in the *pitsya* of his grandmother's gefilte fish but without the smell. So David resolved to investigate for himself.

He donned his sandals and walked to downtown Gomorrah for a visit to the Apikoros nightclub, where a dybbuk who was named Lenny Bruce caused the laughter of apostates into the cold night. But Philistine bouncers turned David from the door of the theater, for he had no money to enter.

Did not they see that his own name would one day adorn the marquee? No, they did not. But they did see him when he tried to sneak in through the kitchen, and they turned him out again with angry voices and upraised fists. Did not they see that they were interfering in God's divine wish? David asked. No, they did not, they replied, adding that he should knock it off already with the Yoda syntax and get out of there before they beat him into chum.

Lo and indeed and verily and other words used to call attention to something important, this was the next step of God's mystery plan—which had been hatched without David's knowledge or signature (which was protocol for all His plans): Force David to earn his way into the theater. How? Emotion. Ambition. Desire. Pride. In other words, all the usual tortures.

Outside the theater, David was anguished. Yet he refused to cry out for God's help, still believing that he was operating beneath His radar, where he intended to stay until the five-alarm blaze in his loins had been extinguished. For whatever other advantages it may offer, the constant companionship of the Lord God Almighty could not possibly be conducive to scoring. It was one thing for Catholic school girls to wear crosses around their necks, which apparently had an aphrodisiacal effect on them; it would be quite another to bring Jesus himself on the date—and worse yet if his Father tagged along. Their plaid-skirt knees would slam shut faster than a post office window at the stroke of five.

Thus did David find work instructing youngsters at Temple Beth Pilpul not in the ways of the Torah or Mishnah or Gemara but in the works of Aleichem.* They sang

---

* Given that no Chicago-area synagogue would have me, I taught Hebrew at Temple Beth El in Gary, Indiana. Three times a week for two and a half years, I rode the Illinois Central there and back—and thought of absolutely nothing while staring out the window.

and danced their way through *Fiddler,* and because it was in the mother tongue, which their parents did not understand, their parents were delighted, which in turn delighted Rabbi Tsuriss, who had not previously been so delighted with David's reform instruction techniques but now tendered him a continued employment contract that included a piece of the action.

Not that David cared, but thus did David please the Almighty with his wiles. Far more importantly, thus did David net enough capital to visit Lenny Bruce at the Temple of the Willingly Damned.

8

avid watched Lenny Bruce pace the stage.* The comedian who dressed like the prime minister of India spake in humor but without jokes. This was modern. There were no horses walking into bars, or priests playing golf with rabbis. The comedian spake, "People ask me how come you guys killed Christ. I tell 'em I don't know, it was just one of those parties that got out of hand. Or I say we killed him 'cause he didn't want to be a doctor. You know, if Jesus had been killed twenty years ago, Catholic kids would be walking around with little electric chairs around their necks instead of crosses."

---

* The first time I saw Lenny Bruce perform was at the Gate of Horn nightclub. The Chicago police, cleverly intuiting that Bruce was swearing in Yiddish, brought in a Yiddish-speaking cop, who arrested him and later testified in court that what the comedian said on stage was obscene. Who knew there were Yiddish-speaking cops?

David sat with his mouth wide agape, like a hungry plague frog, hearing the gales of laughter cascade from his gorge. He had not been so moved by meeting God Himself.* This was funny stuff, and it made the people in the club feel delighted. Many of them, anyway, but not all—for the righteous clapped hands over their ears and muttered rhetorical pieties as they fled in terror of damnation. The others remained and communed as one with the comedian, spitting their two-drink minimums like Danny Thomas spraying coffee from his cup over Marjorie Lord when Rusty Hamer runs in to say that an antelope is loose in the living room.

So what could be bad about the comedian's utterances, which sounded like Spillane hopped up on speed, even if some of the words were said to be forbidden? Indeed, did not the original 613 commandments prohibit many otherwise ordinary activities, like the sowing of different seeds in the same field? Surely His peoples who lived under the yoke of the 613 became eventually conscious that there had been mistakes made in the law, like being unable to consummate love orally in a moving vehicle if thou art the one driving; and surely God Himself belatedly came to the same conclusion, for in His *Reader's Digest* condensed version of only ten commandments, none of them said anything about the sowing of seeds—except to prohibit sowing yours in your neighbor's wife—nor about the uttering of "fuck." They had not, it turns out, been written in stone after all.

---

* God's feelings were hurt, but it went with the territory. He had, after all, designed women to find death-row inmates sexier than salesmen who make a nice living in the suburbs.

David hid in the shadows after the show, to confirm that the comedian with two first names would be rewarded with more than laughter and applause, which to David would have been *dayenu*. And soon he saw the filthy lucre exchange hands. Manna!

But there was yet more: the throaty promises of cocktail waitresses who were stacked like the twin peaks of Mount Sinai and Mount Ararat, both women fighting to expose the grandeur of their lush gold bosoms to him, as well as the wet willingness of their fertile crescents. Neither was willing to concede her place in the comedian's saddle to the other.

"You bitch," came the cry, followed by "I'll scratch your eyes out," as the unclean women, which is the kind of clean preferred by eight out of ten men, drew ready to slay each other. At the last moment, the professional comedian with a fistful of filthy lucre stayed their hands and exhibited the wisdom of Solomon, or at least the libido of David (see: both King and Steinberg). He put the lucre in his pocket and a hand on each of their deuteronomies, and left for the kingdom of heaven on earth, where all three cried God's name until dawn.

David returned the next night and heard more bays of laughter and saw the comedian with two first names receive more money and more unclean women, then did the same the next night and the night after, enough nights in all to know that the comedian's capital could fill a goatskin and that his pleasure might never be filled. But then, why should it have to be when there were even clean women begging him to do whatever was necessary to bestow on them the prefix *un-*. And miracle of miracles, the comedian wasn't even a looker. Nor did that Nehru jacket slake their desire for him. Hallelujah, comedians had groupies.

For David, it was as if the future had beckoned to him seductively with the crook of a beautiful finger. He would follow this temptress anywhere. But by what mode of transport was he to get there? And where would he get the carfare? Such were his metaphors of desire.

9

~*~

God was pleased to see that the young man David had at last discovered ambition, and He took note of David's plight—hungering to be a comedian but not knowing how to advance beyond the free amusement of friends or the taking of doughnuts from seminarians in exchange for explaining the gags in *Summa Theologica*.* Being divine, He of course could have suggested in that sensationally stentorian voice which was

---

* Each morning I would sneak into Swift Hall, the common room of the Chicago Theological Seminary, where payment for food was on the honor system. I quickly learned to punish them for their foolishness by jiggling the coins in the basket as though I'd dropped some in (as opposed to taking some out), then smiling beatifically at the theologians and getting the hell out of there (so to speak) before they caught on. It would be two years before they did. Years later, when I was in Chicago to perform, I snuck into the Hall, dropped a twenty in the basket, and let them keep the change.

itself worthy of Broadway, "First, David, learn stagecraft and the essentials of performance."

But no, for He had come to understand David well and understood that such advice would have been counter-productive. He could hear David saying, "God, don't make me laugh—You should pardon the expression. I mean, not to put too fine a point on it, God, but what do You know about comedy? Sure, if I wanted to be Barrymore, maybe I'd take a meeting. Tragedy, you're good at. But comedy, that's not really Your metier."

To which God could have pointed out, quite rightly, that He had been the Cosmic Author of the whole enchilada, from anguish to belly laughs, irony included (which He'd created on the eighth day, when He waked refreshed from the day off without anything to do). But there was no point trying to explain the joke to one who did not get it, for He Himself had authored the law that a joke explained is a laugh denied. No, it was essential that David believe that he had discovered the route to success himself. So God said nothing, at least not directly. Anyway, He wanted to keep His presence a secret from David, to preserve the illusion that David had given Him the slip. Otherwise He risked overexposure. *Some day,* God thought, *and that day may never cometh, I will call upon David to do Me a service.* And should that day come, God did not want David to suffer from commandment fatigue. Besides, He had also sponsored and signed the universal law about no good deed going unpunished.

God was wise in His plan. He made a deal with the university's admissions director. In exchange for getting to live without a face covered in boils, the director consented to violate university policy by admitting six beautiful coeds, thereby bringing the university's total of beautiful coeds to six. Overnight, all six discovered that they were theater arts majors. They also found themselves adorned in black turtleneck sweaters, tight black skirts with black stockings, their long ponytails sashaying like the tails of ponies in heat, their perfume Eau de Fuck Me—which is to say that these Sirens had the power of Circe to turn men into pigs. Though of course it was the men's own wands that performed the magical swining.

David held tight to himself with both hands and two knees as they passed him in order that the glory of his manhood not fill the espresso house where he was reading Proust for comedy tips, but was catapulted from his seat as their pheromones made a leash around his neck and yanked. Unable to resist, he followed them out the door— a door unseen by him before, leading to where, he knew not; because why, he knew well. Thus did David arrive at a small theater in an outpost of the school frequented only by Gauloise-smoking women reciting Dickinson and Kerouac and men who knew all the words to *My Fair Lady*.

David hid in the shadows of the theater, as he had before when observing the comedian with two first names, and watched the six beautiful coeds and other unbeautiful coeds take direction from a man in rehearsal of a play about a deluded, randy bastard, a syphilitic doctor moonlighting as a philosopher, and a young woman who sleeps with any man (even a rich Jew) who'll pay her rent, the action against a backdrop of torture, murder, and catastrophe—in short, a biblical comedy.

"I'd make a great Candide," David said to himself, seized

suddenly with a desire to act, though he would have to wait until rehearsal ended before declaring his intentions.

With aspirations as enlarged as his manhood, which was going on hour four now as a stiffie, thus putting it dangerously close to the time when medical care is considered advisable, David waited until the six departed and then approached the director, the man called Benedetti.* David proclaimed to him that he had long wished for a life on the stage.

How long? Benedetti asked to know.

"Oh, who can remember that far?" David said, feinting with a line from the play which he had read in the presence of the great Bellow: "It's the best of all possible worlds." He smiled the smile that bespoke charm and an awareness of irony. But Benedetti was not yet moved by the ardor of David's aspiration and did not smile in kind.

"What kind of theater are you interested in?" Benedetti was wont to ask.

"Oh, that's easy," said David, summoning the term uttered from Benedetti's lips but mere minutes before. "Chamber theater. Definitely chamber theater."

"Chamber theater, huh? What kind of chamber theater?"

"You know, the usual stereotypical chamber theater. Just regular old chamber theater, the kind I grew up on."

---

* Robert Benedetti was the director of the Court Theatre at the University of Chicago. He later asked me to form a comedy act with him. We performed only once, in a Toronto folk club called the Fifth Peg. The act, it's fair to say, did not work well with the critics, though it got both of us laid that night—and that is, after all, the goal of all live performance from the performer's perspective.

"Mister, uh, Steinberg?"

"David Steinberg."

"Mister Steinberg, chamber theater is a term I invented off the top of my head just this afternoon."

"Yes, of course. I know that. But it's such a perfect phrase to describe a type of theater. It has an idiomatic quality that transcends the boundaries of time and space and convention, capturing as it does the Platonic conception of an artistic experience that emboldens and enriches us, performer and audience alike, as though—"

"Mr. Steinberg."

"Yes."

"You're a liar."

"Well, there's lying and then there's lying."

"Those are the first true words from your mouth."

"They are?"

"Mr. Steinberg, acting is about lying to serve the truth. If you lie convincingly enough, you will find the truth of the moment and convey it to an audience that rewards authenticity."

"You mean, like George Reeves."

"Who?"

"Superman."

"That's supposed to be funny?"

"No, he makes me believe he can fly."

Benedetti sighed the sigh of Nebuchadnezzar upon learning that his favorite wife could not spell his name, causing him to destroy the Temple, slaughter thousands, and overwater his hanging gardens. Thus spake Benedetti in exasperation, "You're wasting my time."

"But I'm an excellent liar," David insisted. "The best

there is. Ask my parents. Ask anyone I grew up with. Ask Bellow. Ask Roth. Nobody lies like I do. I can lie about anything."

"As I see, Mr. Steinberg. But as you say, there's lying and then there's lying—and this program has no room for cheats, manipulators, charlatans, or connivers. Try the ethnic studies department."

These were the last words that the man Benedetti spoke to David with great forcefulness before making haste to depart, offering no pause for David to cry out in protest or make a burnt offering in sacrifice.

But God was with him. And on his side. Which is not always the case when God is with you, as Jimmy Swaggart discovered when God fingered him in that motel with the hooker and then called the media.

The man Benedetti stopped suddenly as God had silently commanded, paused to think the thought that He had planted in his head, then turned to confront David in order to ask the question that the Almighty, blessed be He, had written on his tongue: "Are you straight, by any chance?"

"My God, yes," David answered with a truthfulness unparalleled in his experience, wondering whether he might be served by explaining the causation of his unrelentingly tumescent member. "You have no idea."

"Well why didn't you say so?" said the man Benedetti, who in his professional capacity had never before met a male of the species who did not plan to make cosmetology his fallback position in case the whole theater thing didn't pan out. "Welcome to the group."

Thus did David invest in a black turtleneck and beret.

10

David scored with the Sirens, as he had hoped. Though he had expected to score with all six at once, in time he scored with all six sequentially, each the other knowing that each the other desired also to spit in the face of bourgeois virginity. A man of black skin would have been a less bourgeois choice, true, but a man with no foreskin served the purpose well enough. And it was good. For none of them had ever met a male who did not esteem the subtext of Judy Garland's oeuvre, and so they eagerly revealed to him the grandeur of their magnificent bosoms and allowed him to bait his hook on the catch-and-release plan in their fertile crescents, as though each had been in training for employment as cocktail waitresses—which without a doubt they were as theater majors. And David gave thanks to God for his good fortune, though he did not mean that literally. Now, if only he could convince the Sirens to see how bourgeois was simple one-on-one intercourse.

And so did *The Caine Mutiny* rehearsals conclude, with the other unbeautiful women also yearning to unburden their remnants of virginity on the sole male in the department who refused to consider the virtues of exfoliation. Alas, David had not the time for amour, he apologized, recommending that they consult Professor Roth, whom he felt certain would offer them succor, particularly the shiksas. Thus did David tell the truth twice in one utterance, a wonder whose rareness he might have paused to admire in contemplation had not he been rushing, he having miscalculated the time remaining before opening night, which indeed came far before he was capable of reciting his lines as they had been written.

Three hours turned out not to be enough to memorize them all. For three hours was just enough time to read the play this first time and draw yellow highlights over his lines, of which he had far more than he had had during his bar mitzvah Torah portion of Leviticus 15, which declaims the necessity of bathing after man lies with woman and proffers an emission of semen. And that much took David seven months to get down cold because he had to keep locking himself in his bedroom with a copy of *Babylon Today* every time he spoke the words aloud, the vision of him and Esther Rambam getting the better of him and his manhood every time. Indeed, as he read the script David was astounded to discover that *The Caine Mutiny* was not concerned with the adolescent rebellion of Abel's brother against his parents for getting them tossed out of a nicer neighborhood.

Up went the curtain, and out came the actors, and on went the play, and the assembled congregation that included the writer Bellow and the university president and two congressmen and one senator and all their mistresses believed the scripted lies to be real and true; and the pin drop echoed in their silence; and all was well in the house until David entered stage right with a brain as empty as Isaac's bladder after he saw Abraham raise the knife (see: Kierkegaard's *Fear, Trembling, and Incontinence*).

Not a word found his lips.

Thus did David, son of Yascha and Ruth, stare into the writer Bellow's eyes, and he could grasp that Bellow waited fixedly, as the woman next to him waited keenly, as rows one through nine waited but without adverbs, as all the congregants waited in the remaining rows, eager, anticipating, hungry for his lines so that the play might draw nearer to the time when they could applaud with cool university disdain and then repair for some coffee and a little cake. They sat forward in their seats without amusement, vowing that next time they will stay home in their pjs and watch the filmed version on *Million-Dollar Movie*.

But those who waited with the most impatience and were least in amusement with David were his fellow actors, especially the Sirens (playing in drag for this male-centric production), whose lips drew back in snarls as they imagined disagreeable notices in the morning papers and foresaw their own subsequent future as cocktail jockeys. Other actors whispered prompted lines to him, but the words coming all at once sounded like that first morning at the Tower of Babel when God pulled off the practical joke of the confusion of tongues—and chaos, not hilarity, ensued. Then the actor named Shtuss in the guise of the character called Queeg viciously hurled the steel ball bearings he held as props toward David's forehead, in an intended reenactment of Goliath's demise. But they did not strike their mark.

Oh, much attention was focused on David. Much detestation did he sense. Much torment did he experience. Thus did he cry out—though silently (of course), keeping the words inside him—"Oh, God, forsake me not," before invoking the capitalized pronoun as additional incentive: "May You answer my prayers that I might serve You better."

Better? God stifled a laugh, for David had not been serving Him at all. No matter, though, for He had no intention of forsaking David, as this was part of His Rube Goldberg plan—as indeed all of His plans could be described.

"Oh, God," cried David some more. "Deus ex machina, deus ex machina—literally. May I either remember my goddamn lines or will You at least open the ground so that it swallows me whole."

Neither of those scenarios came immediately to pass.

Bereft, David now fell to his knees, at least in his mind, and for a human moment God was moved by David's misery and desired to call out in response, "I am here, David, and your line is, 'Hi.'"

11

No, He resisted.

Indeed, resisting such impulses was something that God had become expert at since Leviticus, when He stopped working the crowd and began playing Where's Waldo. Though it is true that He felt varying degrees of affection for most (all right, some) of His people, He understood that to answer their prayers too many times too directly would threaten the delicate Greek-tragedy balance between faith, confusion, and farce that He had worked so hard to achieve over the centuries with a series of abominable slaughters and incomprehensible wrongs leavened by tiny justices that people call miracles—like falling in love or a lost cat showing up after three months or candles that burn a few days longer than predicted.

So let them call His ways mysterious. Of course they're mysterious. What the hell else should they be? Obvious? Get a clue. Anyone who thinks that isn't thinking through the consequences of His people getting a backstage glimpse at that which is better left unseen in God's sausage factory. Who, after all, turns to the last page in Agatha Christie before reading the rest? If He let them in on the plan, they'd be bored with the rest of their miserable little lives, or else paralyzed by fear, or else eager to abandon whatever remained of civility. Better the believers should call Him mysterious and the unbelievers try to connect dots between butterflies flapping in Calcutta and hurricanes in Port St. Lucie. Whatever gets them through the night is all right by Him.

But enough already with the devout assholes who brag in happy times that they "know" God but then suddenly lose their faith in Him after something bad happens to them personally. *Hello!* Were not they paying attention to newspapers and history books? Billions dead for no apparent reason across the millennia, but now that they themselves are taking it in the shorts, God is either a figment or has let them down? That's so goddamned typical of His people. No wonder He can't trust them with The Secret.

Yes, there was a moment once when He got fed up with that momzer Hymie Aroysgevorfen hondling Him to win the lottery. Week after week, year after year, the same old mantra, "God, please let me win. I'll never ask for anything else again." Finally, He could stand it no more and instead of giving the little shit cancer so that he'd have something more substantial to pray about, He spoke aloud to Hymie. He said, "Schmuck, meet me halfway: At least buy a ticket."

And yes, He sometimes regretted having told His messengers to tell His people to go forth and multiply, because they had done that quite well—too well, alas. Things were so much quieter back when there were billions fewer of His people; the prayers were not nearly as plentiful or loud. That was the day before Sammy Finkelstein came up with that infernal saying, "From your mouth to God's ears," which soon caught on and became the tipping point for prayer saturation (as well as the reason why Sammy lived out his days as an organ grinder's monkey).

Sometimes, especially in winter and during downturns in the economy, the racket is unbearable, even for the One who can bear an unbearable racket (though He cannot yet construct a four-sided triangle). God this and God that, they cry. God God God please please please I beg You I beg You I beg You. And so on—plus, they thank Him constantly. "Thank God," they say for the smallest stupidest things, especially when they don't mean it. Oh, and then they ask Him to forbid things. "Oy," they say, "God forbid." Apparently, nothing's too small for Him to forbid, like a son not getting into an Ivy. And then when the boy does get in, they thank Him again (even if they don't need it—because *their* boy, well, he didn't need any help from Him).

True, He had commanded them, time and again, to LOVE Him, dammit, with all their heart and soul and to cleave to His ways. But Who do they think He is, a celestial butler? Had not He given them free will? They only use it to get in trouble—and then dial up the Big Fella to bail them out. Even His unlisted number and registration in the "do not call" database cannot keep away the entreaties. After all these millennia, He has heard them all—prayers for money, sex, hair, the 3–6–4 trifecta, even peace. Apparently there is nothing people will not pray for.

And that, you will want to know, was what had attracted God to David in the first place: the affectionate way David studied Him but without expecting swag in return, which even dear Mother Teresa had sometimes requested—soap for the feet of beggars, rain for the parched crops, a new schmatte now and then for her head (oh, and that Nobel, which He happily arranged). But, except for Esther Rambam's cherry in exchange for his own—which was the kind of prayer that did not count against a young man's tally—David had requested nothing special.

Until now.

The fact that the young man was doing so publicly and loudly was a little surprising to Him until God remembered that, had He not revealed Himself to David, David would not now be calling to Him in such an annoying way. So it was therefore His fault, and He took responsibility for His actions, which was more than He could say for most of His people.

It's all right, David, He thought, *for this is all part of My plan.*

12

"Oh, dear God, why have you forsaken me?" David cried, but even as he spake the words he grokked that it was he who had forsaken God. Well, not forsaken Him, exactly; more like not RSVP'ed to Him for a while, which is technically not forsaking. But what madness, what folly, had he committed? Here God had offered His hand in divine friendship, and David had slapped It away. Who in history had ever refused God's meet-and-greet like that?

True, God had come on a little too strong, like a squeegee man near the West Side Highway off-ramps, and David would have probably paid better attention if God had been a little less on the nose and sent, say, a talking donkey in His place, as He had with that shtunk prophet Balaam. Hey, a talking donkey— that's not something you see every day. Which was why David had so enjoyed those Francis movies with Donald O'Connor and not Ingrid Bergman's Joan of Arc. Anyone can talk to God. From a talking donkey, a franchise can be built.

But Jesus, shouldn't God be a bigger god than that? Didn't that kind of put him on the same level as Zeus and Odin? Was this really quid pro quo—you ignored Me so I abandon you? David tried to feel angry at God for being so damned petty, but his heart would not follow. The worship he suddenly felt for God reminded him of that sixth-grade dance where he had suddenly tired of Amy Zipperstein and cast her off among wallflowers, later to see her dancing nose to nose with that miserable little poseur, Jerry Schwartzfeld. Just like that, she had been transformed in David's eyes into a vision every bit as lilting as the Red Sea closing on Pharaoh's men, and in a fit of jealousy David threatened to hack off his rival's payess and knock him back to Chelm, or wherever he came from—but, surprise, Amy had stood with Jerry against David.

Wait a minute. Had that really happened to him, or had David just imported a Joe Tex song into his own personal experience—part of the synesthesia of imagination and memory that had accompanied him since childhood, which was what made him such an accomplished liar: "You'd better hold on to what you've got. 'Cause if you think nobody wants it, just throw it away and you will see, someone will have it before you can count *aleph, bet, gimmel.*" No, this had actually happened to him—the point being that David had not appreciated his good fortune until it had been lost to him. Thus was it now with God, who in fact had authored that tendency into His people.*

---

* As any English major with a minor in philosophy now earning his living as a Quiznos manager will attest, this is a basic tenet of Western civilization.

David shouted one final cry of anguish over the notion of the Almighty watching His sunset on the beach with someone new ("Can you make it a little more purple? Perfect, thank You. More Manischewitz?"), then rose to his feet, aware that as he was now, so would he be always: pitifully, miserably, excruciatingly alone in the universe. It was entirely without consolation to know that at least God existed, which most people would consider a nugget of ecstasy. But not David, not now. Indeed, he thought it far worse to have known Him and then to have lost Him, as this gaping chasm in David's soul was never again to be filled with anything but grief from the loss of hosting the Lord.

I didn't realize he was such a drama queen, thought God.

And now David faced his audience, and from that gaping chasm in which his neon vacancy sign seemed destined to glow forever, just like the one at Bates Motel, rose clarity of thought and speech born of the realization that he had only himself to rely on and had only laughter to offer the world:

"Booga booga," proclaimed David, "booga booga."

David had at last spoken, so there was deliverance from the void of silence, but what were these words that he spake? Had they been remembered from the text or were they to be found in the midrash? Or did these words originate somewhere new and unexpected?

There followed a moment of confounded silence from the audience and cast whose eyes yet bore into him as they pondered the mystery. And then there appeared a sweet burst of giggle from the aisle on row 14, followed by a chortle from the balcony, a chuckle from down front, and snorts from SRO. Soon did the whole room shake with laughter—for laughter is a contagion, even on those who think not that something is funny; indeed, a grin appeared even on the writer Bellow, who had no notes.

And the laughter continued and grew with every new lie uttered—and they were clean lies, white lies, smart lies, lies considered by the audience to be hilarious. And David knew not from whence they came, but come they did.

Remember that chasm of pain and despair? Neither did David.*

Thus was God pleased. He loves it when a Plan comes together.†

------

* The performance took place in the law auditorium at the University of Chicago. A reviewer from the school newspaper, *The Maroon*, would write: "As the lawyer Barney Greenwald, Mr. Steinberg is unbelievable!"

† I naturally tried on the second night to remember and re-create what I'd done the first night—and discovered that no such thing is possible. There soon arose from the audience the greatest collective yawn in the history of mankind, and by the second-act curtain no one was left in the auditorium.

13

⸙

The director Benedetti made way toward David after
the falling of the stage curtain, which a stagehand
had tried without victory to make land fatally on
David's head. But he could not advance easily, for there
was a great throng of actors in the region of David, and
it was a great tumult, and they were attempting to smite
him with fists and scenery and props and steel ball bearings, and they were having success. They were, it seems
safe to say, angry with David, for he had gone off script
but never back on script. This had caused the actors who
were now angry with him to have no value in their roles
for which they had studied and memorized and rehearsed
and taken direction in the worship of becoming someday
rich and famous and beloved and sated sexually beyond all
imagination; and now had come David to pace the stage
for an hour and ignore the holy text and reduce them all
to spear carriers as he made billows of laughter to appear

from the audience—laughter instead of the tears for the captain Queeg who was not permitted to unravel slowly but rather to glare and mope and seethe and wish along with the rest of the cast for David to die screaming alone in a leper colony.

David did not cry out for God to deliver him from the pummeling, for he believed that God had abandoned him and that, anyway, not even God could hear him over the crashing applause (applause that tasted sweeter than the blood from his nose). Of course, he was blissfully unaware of God's presence in the scheme behind the laughter that he had caused to come from those spectators who had wet themselves gladly at his utterances.

David thought not that his utterances had been, relatively speaking, deserving of such laughter. He thought that such had burst forth from the people because he had delivered them from a night that had promised not rich dramatic reward but instead the hope of a good impression and, God willing, tenure. For on this night they had expected to witness, yet again, plot and dialogue which they had seen on Broadway, and if not on Broadway then in the moving pictures—and instead had come David, whose unexpected words roused them from their sleepy torpor and made them have hysterics, for the change in program was blessedly welcome.

And, deserved or not, welcome was to David the sound of laughter. Yes, welcome, welcome, welcome it was— beautiful laughter, as welcome and enticing as the spread legs of a young beauty. Maybe more welcome, in fact; more welcome and more enticing and more addictive. All right, probably not *more* welcome, etc. Anyway, why compare the two? Can't live without one, don't want to live without the other now. Undeserved? Irrelevant. After all, does not a boy who lies for his first time with a streetwalker learn to love poontang just as well as the virgin groom on his wedding night?

The actors, led by Queeg, continued pummeling David but tired quickly of the exertion (except for Queeg) and so decided instead to stone him using a size of rock guaranteed to inflict maximum hurt before the protracted death, and they were preparing to do so when the director Benedetti finally advanced into view.

The actors parted for Benedetti in the joyous expectation that the director whose name ended in a vowel would be furiouser even than they were at David for the desecration of his temple and would hence plant a kiss on David's lips to signify that friends of Benedetti whom he called "the boys" would soon fit David with a pair of cement shoes and make him to lie with the fishes at the bottom of Lake Michigan. Which was a perfect solution, for then none of them would have to take up residence at a penal complex but yet David would receive his just reward for fucking up their lives so utterly.

The director Benedetti held David's bleeding cheeks and appeared to make ready to plant the kiss of betrayal that signified that David was a dead man walking. Instead, he said first to David, "There's a word for what you did tonight? Do you know what it is, David?"

"Suicide?"

"No, improv."

"Improv?"

"Yes, improv."

David was not known with the word *improv,* just as

he had not been known with the word *comedian*. *Improv* was not a true word but rather an abbreviation of *improvisation*—the art and science of making shit up as you go along, and it was apparently not a skill that blessed vast swaths of His people.

Said the director, "You have a God-given talent," to which David replied, "You have no idea."

Now then did the director plant a kiss on David. But it was not the kiss of betrayal; it was a kiss of affection. And the actors who had prayed for the kiss of slow torturous death had now to smile with bravery and to go off script and be actors better than they had been given an opportunity to be that night in their pretending that they were also delighted with the performance of David and with laughter for him from those idiots in the gallery. But most of all they had to pretend delight with the esteem for David of their director, whom they must yet please for the rest of the season but who until this moment they did not know shared the IQ of a lentil. What of that vowel ending his name? Did not it entitle them to a triple-word-score's worth of revenge? And where was his rage at dishonor? For they could see plainly that he had none. Now came another kiss and an arm around the shoulder as he escorted David through the throng of actors, who fell to the stage floor prostrate in a pique of woe and geshrying.

The blood from David's nose began suddenly to trickle backward, and the puffiness around his eyes from the blows went down a little, though not as much as if he had applied cold cucumber slices, which sometimes works for Elizabeth Taylor in the morning.

Said the director Benedetti, "I'm taking you to see the guys."

"The guys?"

And now there came famine in David's soul as the two words bespoke the promise of unpleasant consequences. And now did the others who heard those words too rise to their feet and rejoice in the knowledge that the sly director Benedetti had been keeping his friends close but his enemy closer and was now going to hand David two tickets to Vegas and escort him out to the car where fat Clemenza in the backseat would make "Hello, David" the last words David would ever hear before the circumcising of his throat. David wondered if God would save him from this fate. No, David decided, He would not, for He had obviously abandoned him; and he lamented not having virgin teenage daughters, so he could pimp them out as a payoff, the way Lot had tried to bribe Sodom's angry villagers to just go away.

14

But it came to pass that "the guys" meant not "the boys." And indeed the director Benedetti's boys were children, not goombahs.* And the guys were other actors of youth and wit known to Benedetti whom he admired and who received a bit of lucre for their talent at devising without script an evening of bacchanalian laughter for an audience that had arrived to the theater not for Aristotelian poetics or possible tenure but for the purpose of laughing, which they did much of without knowing much and more of if they were also acquainted with words like *Aristotelian* and *bacchanalian*.

And the funny actors called themselves "Second City."

---

* Actually, it was not Benedetti who introduced me to Second City. It was Bill Alton, director of the University of Chicago theater and a founding member of the troupe, who deserves the blame. I prefer to tell the story this way, because Benedetti is a funnier name.

And some of them were bound for glory in their skill. And some of them had already achieved glory, performing a type of stage entertainment known as skits that were not rehearsed but which made themselves known to the performers' imaginations when revelers in the audience exclaimed words of suggestion like "King Kamehameha" and "syntopicon" and "Jack the Ripper" and "repression." And there were no props or punch lines to aid them in this improv, only the terrifying beauty of nothingness which they filled with Creation and structure, just as God once had, but going Him one or two better, for they had humor and no wrath in their structures. And these were some of their names to celebrate: Mike Nichols, Elaine May, Alan Arkin, Barbara Harris, Jack Burns, Avery Schreiber, Joan Rivers, Severn Darden, Paul Sand, Dick Schaal, Fred Willard, Robert Klein. And their spawn are too many to name, and so are the spawn of their spawn, so that their progeny yet to this day bring forth merriment and pleasure on three continents.

Now then, at the temple of the Second City in a building that they called a theater, did David sit in an audience and observe the actors in their talent. And he wept with joy and admiration for the glory of their genius at turning lies into laughs—the pretend tour of an art museum with invisible paintings, the pretend fitting by a tailor of a buxom woman, the pretend talk between a policeman and a man about to jump from a building.

All pretend, all lies, all laughter, all the time.

And they called it work? Hah! This was how David had been lying all his days; and for free; and sometimes suffering punishments for it.

Why had not he known of this sub rosa world before now? For it was here, in this synagogue of mirth, that congregants rose to worship the true lies, which had the effect to make true liars holy—which in that case would place David somewhere in the holiness hierarchy between Moses and Abraham.

Knowing blissfully not that he had been maneuvered to this place by the Hand of the Almighty Puppeteer, David contemplated joining this congregation—if they would have him and his talent.

And in the contemplation of the joining he felt more overjoyed than had the first Hebrews to check in to the promised land.

This was his destiny, David believed, to lie for a living.

Only then, hearing laughter that he had caused, would life with all of its horrors and terrors and built-in obsolescence and despair and misery and loneliness still be a suitable way to pass time.

Thus did David enjoy the same inspiration that had moved Sarah at age ninety, when she birthed a child for the first time and named him "He shall laugh"—Isaac. Though of course, after being the first-ever guest of honor at a bris and surviving that episode of binding on Mount Moriah, Isaac never really developed into much of a laugher. In this paradox, he was not unlike the girl Chastity whom David went home with after the show.

15

David inquired about paying dues to join the Temple of Second City. But they turned him away, for the membership was full and they knew not his work. Nor did they care to know his work. Nor, frankly, did he have work. It was said that if they opened the door to him, then they would have to open the door to other knocks of other comedy seekers, and then there would be no room on the stage for any skits other than subway conversations at rush hour, and no one in the audience to pay and watch and laugh. Besides, they had noticed David at twenty-seven consecutive performances, which struck them as creepy and obsessive, and when they ran an audit they found that he had snuck into every one, meaning they had not been enriched even a little by his lucre.*

---

* I attended so many performances in order to confirm that there was no script for this hilarity, and that the performances varied from one to the next. After all, if I was going to make this a career, I had be sure that there was no memorizing involved.

16

～❦～

God looked down and saw what there was to see, which was David sitting on the curb outside the temple of laughter in a wait for thoughts to become solutions, so God sent a servant called Gene to David as a solution.

One moment Gene was before a jury, arguing that his client be not banished from Eden for the crime of stealing apples (a truckload of them, as well as the truck and the driver—at gunpoint, wearing a mask, with two priors), and the next moment Gene was beside David, declaring that what he really wanted to do was direct.

"Hey, kid," Gene asked, "do you want to put on a funny show?"

David said sure, and then God booked them into a small theater on favorable terms and packed the theater with patrons and watched anonymously from the back and laughed along with everyone else, for they were amusing.* And then He made to laugh with gusto a newspaper reviewer whom He had comped with house seats; and in the early morning hours He guided the reviewer's hands on the keyboard, whispering to him as He had to Moses; and indeed this turned out to be the best writing He'd ever done, commandments included (most of them, anyway). Proudly, He showed it off to the city of Chicago, making certain that the newspaper was opened to the review page when it fell on the stoops of the Second City actors (just as He would later draw clock hands on page A20 of Bob Woodward's *New York Times* when He wanted to drop some Watergate clues).

And the actors read the review, which was good ink and said, "Second City should see these guys"—which was as close to divine coercion as He wanted to get in this matter. But it was enough and it worked, and the Second City actors were as overjoyed as cart owners had been after the wheel's invention.

The actors remembered their rudeness to David and begged his forgiveness and implored him to join their congregation.

And he did, and it was good, and God did not mind David's musing that his impressive string of successes, including prodigious amounts of loveless sex, had begun the moment David chose to abandon God, for He saw the events through David's eyes, and exactly did it appear

---

* Gene Kadish and I, billed as Kadish and Steinberg, opened at Old Town North and played for two weeks before moving next door to a bigger venue where we opened for Oscar Brown, Jr., and then Robert Clary. Brown and Clary both went on to success. Kadish is now a successful lawyer in Phoenix. And me?

so—for indeed, this was all detailed and accounted for in His plan.

Thought David, *I think God was bad luck for me. And you know what else? I bet I woulda scored with Esther Rambam way back when if I hadn't been so focused on God's teachings. I think He was like some kind of body odor.*

Maybe, David thought, he would now write to Esther and invite her to come to Chicago and see him on stage; and in seeing him up there she would be as a willing vixen to him, with her now twenty years of ripeness, and reveal to him the moist warm secrets of her lush gold womanness. And if he was really lucky she will have not yet known a man in this way, though of course there were also significant advantages if she indeed had already known a man, especially one who knew a thing or two about ripe young booty and he was patient and skilled in tutoring where to put what and how to shake that thang. But if she had met such a man—who was this asshole and why had she willingly borne her velvet secrets to him first, that shtunk, and not to David, he who would have lied to half of Winnipeg in exchange for just one little peek?

No matter, though, David thought, for now he will have home-court advantage. And she will revel in the laughter that he causes to come from the people. And it will be truer and louder and more musical laughter than the ordinary laugh that she is used to, which is from the eternally funny noise of wind breaking unexpectedly in a crowded Canadian elevator. And this will have an impact on her, he hoped, and make her twitter helplessly as well. And she will fall breathlessly on Table 6 after hours in order to have him take her right then and there, and acquaint him wholly and totally with her lush grandeur, for she will think of him as that rarest of men—one who smells of danger, as all show business people do, and yet makes a living and can get reservations at the last minute on a Saturday night.

But *wait a second,* thought David. *This suddenly reminds me of Faust. I gave up God and all of a sudden I'm getting everything I wanted, and a lot of stuff I didn't even know I wanted but it's good stuff, I can't lie, and I hope it keeps on coming, but it does seem a little fishy. Doesn't it? I mean, what are the chances that this kind of stuff happens all on its own?*

Such was the U-turn in his thinking.

Christ, what a run I'm on. Nobody's ever had a run like this, except maybe Scott Baio. Hmm. I wonder if I really did somehow make a deal with the devil. Is that possible? Is that the only explanation for why I'm getting laid like crazy and scoring points in my chosen field, even though I just chose the field ten minutes ago—because the devil owns my soul? How would I know? Where do I go to find out? It's not like there's side effects—headaches, dry mouth, anal discomfort. What a bitch. Maybe I did, but I don't remember signing a contract or anything, so maybe you don't have to sign anything. I mean, I didn't sign up with God, either; it just happened the way it happened all of a sudden one day. So that could be the deal with the devil, too—it's one of those you're-either-with-me-or-against-me Manichean kind of things. Maybe there's no middle ground in the universe. Maybe you have to be on one side or the other, even if you don't know it. Maybe when you leave one team you end up as a player to be named later on the other.*

---

* I at last resolved the issue and got a good night's sleep that night after first trying to distill the experience into a haiku. That I was utterly unable to, and also that I caught myself in the zipper of my pants, allowed me to make peace with good fortune—for I was not, it seemed, completely blessed after all.

17

od was delighted with David's rumination, for
it reminded Him of His salad days back in
Mesopotamia, when he was Himself still futz-
ing with the lines of demarcation between good and evil,
and the rules (if any) for punishment and reward—indeed,
whether there would, in fact, be an afterlife, and if there
was, how many VHF channels one could get, depending.
That was why His early humans lived to be 250, or 500,
even older—much longer than they would live to until
the 22nd century—because He could not yet decide what
to do with them after they had shuffled off their mortal
coils. Like cholesterol and rashes and physics, these were
big issues to be resolved and could not be hurried, for they
would impact the whole gestalt of His universe, so He did
the unthinkable and took another day of rest, this time to
sleep on it in hopes of clearing his mind. Actually, He slept
in, and when He woke, He could not find Abel, for Abel

had been murdered by his brother Cain. That caught Him by surprise, and in those days He did not much like surprises. *God damn it,* He thought, *You can't take Your eye off these friggin' Urs for even a minute.* (In those days, He also liked speaking in the second person.)

At the time of the murder, He was still working through whether it would be better and more common for bad things to happen to good people, or good things to happen to bad people. *On one Hand,* He would think. *But on the other. . .* The interruption broke His concentration, so He never resolved that issue, because by the time He figured out what to do with murderers and then got back to good and bad, after the whole heaven-hell-purgatory matter, it had become one of those things that you can't remember why it was so important in the first place—even if you are You—and so He covered His bases with the declaration that became universal law: "Shit happens."

Then did it come to pass that He reluctantly picked up off His nightstand and read the second major work about Him and His times (working title: *The Book of Goyim*), this one not an autobiography, and discovered with delight that it painted a portrait of Him far more pleasing than the one from the book He had dictated to Moses, from which was derived the song sung at the end of Sabbath services calling Him the "dreaded one." Oh, how He had hated that now. Dreaded? Him? That was not how He considered Himself, but that was the image they'd gotten of Him from his own words. Maybe he should've listened to His stenographer, Moses, who'd suggested to Him that They hire an editor for the old book—someone objective who would not be shy to send back to the Author queries in the margin, asking for His clarification, like why He had created scorpions to make miserable their forty desert years, and could not their wandering have been shortened by GPS. The way it was being written, insisted Moses, He ran the risk of appearing petulant and petty and capricious—which were not the most appealing attributes for the Creator of the world Who desires His people to love each other faithfully and true.

Alas, He had not listened. He had let His ego get in the way and pointed out that His people were made in His image and therefore suffered the same foibles as He. Moses countered that argument with the suggestion that, perhaps, if He could cut back just a little on the emotion and twist the truth a teeny bit so as not to seem so, uh, hypercritical and arbitrary and vengeful, His people might feel more inclined themselves not to let petty differences define them. Which was an argument that God had ended with the admonition that they were writing journalism, not hagiography, and that their first obligation was to the truth, no matter where it led.

And thus was it so.

And thus was He dreaded.

But at least He had street cred.

Oh but then, because He is a living God—and not the absentee landlord that Spinoza claimed He was, though the damned heretic had never bothered calling Him for comment—He saw the error of His ways when came the first edition of the New Testament, a major publishing event culled from more than 17,000 submissions sent in by first-time hopeful authors fervent to be published in a book that promised annuity royalties until the End of Days.

Indeed, the *Book of Goyim*'s editors had pored with stakes

of pain over each manuscript but revealed not their stern criteria for selection—which did not include consistency, plausibility, or originality. So there came after the final cut disgruntled grousing from the rejected, who allowed unclean words to pass from their lips, for they could not value why, for example, there had to be four versions of the Son's life; two offerings each from the Thessalonians and Corinthians (word on the road was that the second Corinthian had pledged a generous gift to the building fund); and even a typically vapid offering from the Colossians.

"Jesus Christ," asketh Lefkowitz, "whoever listens to anything a Colossian says? Just Galatians and Ephesians—and they're both in there, too. Just goes to show, you gotta know someone. And how come the Romans get such good billing up top? Better they shoulda called it 'Greeks,' with all the back-door man talk, and I think you know what I mean. Look, if I've told you once, I've told you M times . . . "

Almost from the very first pages, God saw the light. All right, so the theology was a little off (and there were words in it like *thitherward*). Big deal. He would cut the authors some slack on that, for they could not be expected to comprehend the uncomprehendable (sometimes He could barely keep track of it Himself). But what struck Him most was how much kinder and more compassionate and gentler He appeared on these pages than in that older testament of His own authorship. Was this the real Him? Or the Him that He aspired to be? Either way, He blushed—and thus came into being the first episode of global warming.

Oh, it was wonderful, this complete makeover that required not a little airbrushing of history and the introduction of a new hero and scenes of Grand Guignol with martyrs and music and mystery. Yes, He did foresee (and foreview) the potential for terrible violence and hatred and misunderstanding down the line with a few of the book's more impractical notions and its finger-pointing at His Chosen people, for it was destined to be an influential bestseller. But those grim conflicts would surely be beside the point, which was that He enjoyed being thought of as a splendid and loving God, not just a stern, fearsome One. And it went to His Head. Whether He was or was not kinder and more compassionate had no importance, He declared, thus conceiving of and implementing the universal law that perception equals reality. Which explaineth why He fancied the idea of having a perfect son, as portrayed in the book: Because a perfect son tends to reflect well on his Father, no matter which side of the nature-nurture argument you come down on or how loathsome the father (see: JFK).

True, the young man had not really been His son uniquely different from all His other generations of sons and daughters, beginning in Eden. And He was genuinely puzzled why so many of His other children who were themselves acquainted with the story of their ancestors would believe that the Lord God Almighty, who had created the entire world in a mere six days, would need to exercise His power of eminent domain over an unoccupied womb belonging to a woman who was both married and a virgin (uh-huh) in order to fashion a child. Who did they think He was—He who understood the words to "Louie, Louie"—that He would require a full nine months to bring His alleged son into being? It did not make sense, and because it did not, alas, He couldn't be bothered to think through what harm there might be in letting the young man go on pretending to be unique, except insofar as there was grievous harm done directly to the young man himself (who played hurt better than anyone God had ever seen). As grievous harms go, this was bad, no doubt, though not as severe as countless others before him—He was, after all, the Author of plagues, famine, floods, slavery, and torture—and rarely had He intervened in those dramas.

Yea, though, verily, lo, God knew that the young man Jesus was filled with devastation and surprise—as much surprise as that caused by Adam's first orgasm and, much much later, by Eve's first—at the entry of the nails. For he had been well-acquainted with the story of Abraham and Isaac and no doubt expected God to dial the Roman warden at the eleventh hour and stay the executioner's hammer, the way He had for Isaac—who was not even God's son, as he imagined himself to be in that eccentric calculus.

But God also understood His people's nature, for it was His nature, as well. The longer the young man lingered among the living, the more likely it was that he would wear out his welcome and the more likely would be His people to find fault with him and pick at his nits. And then he would not be considered perfect anymore. And then the legend would not become myth. And then the myth could not be printed. And then God could not *qvell* with pleasure over His perfect son and bask in the reflected glory and see His poll numbers go up. They knew not what they did? Pish-posh. They knew, they knew. Thus did He coin the aphorism "Only the good die young"—to cover His tracks. And thus did He declare, "So saith the Lord," which tends to end a lot of otherwise perfectly rational discussions.

But He digressed, as had David. And God, who was

privy to both digressions, marveled at their thematic similarity. His plan to turn David into a professional instrument of laughter—and thus bring additional joy and pleasure to a world that He had ordained would soon be beset by a gap in generations and a culture that would be counter and a war that would be in Vietnam—was, He believed, going swimmingly.

Do not decide that God did not have other business to attend to besides David, though much of the rest seemed uninteresting by comparison—endless readings of petitions followed by pro forma denials, as well as the usual catastrophes and woe. Anyway, the enchilada seemed pretty much to run itself after all these millennia, faults and all, and there was always the option of putting the works on automatic pilot. Giving His people free will had been a stroke of genius, for it allowed Him to get involved as much or as little as He desired. Indeed, He Himself did not know why some people caught His attention more than others, but even the Creator has to have a little mystery in His day, so this was the one He chose not to solve, which explains a great deal about both God and David.

18

And so it came to pass in the Temple of Second City that David was younger than the others, who were older as some aunts and uncles are older, especially the aunts and uncles who spring you out of school early one Wednesday for a surprise trip downtown to smoke hand-rolled cigarettes and drink scotch in strip joints and point out the great rack on that one girl who just passed and ask if you'd like to meet her because you could if you have an extra ten, but warn you on the way home not to tell your mother how you got all jiggy with them. And David showed that he was the type of young man who would not give them up to his mother—even when she smells smoke on his clothes and measures his dilated pupils and scrapes the flaked vomit from his shirt and finds an empty Trojan wrapper in his pocket and is furious with him and demands to know who did this to him and threatens to ground him until he's thirty unless he coughs up the info.

The funny actors experienced that they could trust
David to be with them as adults who are rebellious laugh-
makers, and they shared the spotlight and the applause
with him, for he was funny, too, which they enjoyed. And
all went as David wished it to go, except for the fact that
Esther Rambam did not arrive in Chicago. But instead of
throwing himself on a dunghill and weeping with bitterness in his soul, David lifteth up his pecker to the Sirens
and Vixens and Sontags and others who assembled at the
door of the tabernacle of the congregation with the desire
of acquainting him with their yeast. For laughter and
headlines, it seems, are a powerful offering and a good
get. Highly did they esteem him, leaving him no need
to whisper them pleasant nothings in order to consummate the pleasure. And all was good, and David could say
to his father, "Yes, from this you can make a living" but
without the "God willing" part. And God did not mind
the exclusion.

Now came into the Temple of Second City a man with
a cigar as long as the staff of Moses to make David an
offer that he could not refuse as Pharaoh could not refuse
Moses, though without the bullying of plagues.* And then
was David let go to New York for to star on Broadway with
actors of great skill and experience, though he knew less
about acting than did Pharaoh's general know about tide

---

* My first agent was Harry Kalcheim, who ran the William Morris
Agency with his brothers, Norman Brokaw, and Abe Lastfogel. Here's
one thing you should know about them: in 1971, they posed for a
picture with Secretariat, all of them standing directly under the horse.
Their heads did not reach as high as its stomach.

schedules. And this was the title by which the first play was known: Jules Feiffer's *Little Murders,* a satire of violence that that even the audience soon wanted to commit on its characters, and these were its actors: Elliott Gould and Heywood Broun. And in its entire seated congregation were nine of the populace, of which one was a man of printed newspaper words who seemed not well moved by the work. And the ways of the producers soon grieved for its closing, which it did almost before intermission, for this was a work ahead in years of its time—four years, to be precise.

And this was the name of David's second play: *Carry Me Back to Morningside Heights,* which was a work of sensitivity and timeliness and relevance and high-mindedness and social importance led by a director who was also an actor of great skill and accomplishment and dark skin, and this was his name: Sidney Poitier.* And these were the names of his actors, Cicely Tyson and Louis Gossett, who were also of great skill and dark skin. And the production gave heat into the air, and there was expectation of the play having power to end strife and war and hate and crime and unfair business practices, and to open the door for the messiah's return, though the messiah had yet to make his debut. And it came to pass that among the congregation on that first night sat a man of words having his own rookie night representing a false god before which

---

* At the Variety Club in Philadelphia one night, I was aghast to discover that Sidney Poitier, one of the most elegant men of the last millennium, was perhaps the worst dancer of the last two millennia. In God's world, apparently, you're either elegant or you can dance.

the people of New York and America bowed and prayed, and the name of the false god was *The New York Times*. And though the man who wrote the words needed SPF 90 before venturing into the Midtown sun in January, truly did he declare the play "racist." And verily did the faithful gasp in appreciation of the warning of sin and keep the faith by staying home and therefore remaining shielded from the racism. And thus did the play disappear like Madonna's sense of shame before a camera. But in truth the reviewer had not conceived that word in his notice. His praise for the play were these words: "Absolutely thrilling. One can only hope that *Carry Me* runs forever with this magnificent cast intact"—though these were not the words that appeared in the columns of the false god the following morning; his sentiments had been secretly altered by an invisible hand (hint: Hand), for the Plan was not as the reviewer had wished to indicate, which meant that there was no contest.

And so David made haste to return to Chicago and the Temple of the Second City, unaware that he and Broadway had been punked by God.*

---

* It is my contention that all of my bad reviews over the decades can be similarly explained.

19

hen for a moment did David Steinberg come to the acquaintanceship of an entertainment aspirant who was himself without performing aptitude but who was said to possess a genius for the recognition of such talent in others.* And this he saw, or said he saw, in David. And he used the word *eschatology* correctly in context, though his office was yet adjacent to the mailroom at the time. Oh, David was made an impression on, believing that this man embodied the most excellent qualities of

---

* In all, I spent six years at Second City. After my first year, the *Chicago Sun-Times* reviewer Glenna Syse referred to me as "Chaplinesque." As a consequence, for the next two years I didn't get a single laugh—but insisted on having a spotlight on my ass as I waddled toward the wall. And while I managed to resist the urge to grow a mustache, I did look into joining the Communist Party. (See: J. Edgar Hoover's personal files.)

Adnan Khashoggi and Vin Diesel while demonstrating the nose of a psychic for the next big thing—which fact he had proved by correctly shorting Sonny for Cher. And David, insisted the man, was the next big investment—bigger, hallelujah, than Keith Olbermann. This David enjoyed to hear as he enjoyed to hear supermodels enjoy themselves under him loud enough to get busted for decibel violations. "Let's talk," said the man, "about what it is that *you* want. You tell me what *you* want. Let me hear what I can do for *you*. I'm all about *you*."

These words (which all clients fall for; see: grifters) were pleasant words to hear, almost as pleasant as, "My God, you're hung like a horse." And because of that David's head swam with possibilities as he had a clear answer for the man about exactly what the man could do for *him*: "I heard," said David, "that Mike Nichols is casting a movie about a college graduate who suffers from ennui, so he has an affair with his father's partner's wife, then falls in love with the woman's daughter. I'm perfect for the guy—perfect age, perfect temperament. It's like the part was written for me. So what you can do for *me* is get me a meeting with Nichols. Once he meets me, I'm pretty sure I can get the part."

The man laughed like Victoria Gotti seeing Sam Kinison naked. "*You?*" he explained. "David, come on, I was thinking more like a judge on *Project Runway*. Believe me, I know for a fact that Nichols wants someone tall and hunky, not short and punky. Someone big, muscular, and handsome. Someone to make you drool. My money's on Warren Beatty."

And so did it pass that David did not meet Nichols, and so it did pass that this movie was the only '60s movie in which Warren Beatty did not appear; and its leading light was a novice who came up to here on David and had ten years on the character—and, as was one day later revealed, it was not Nichols but this man who had desired someone tall and hunky with muscles and great pecs to drool over.

Decades would pass before David again exchanged words with this man, whose name was David Geffen and who by then owned everything as far as the eye could see in all directions. Which made him, even God agreed, richer than God.*

---

* David Geffen was indeed my agent in 1968. If only he had given me a little less career advice and instead offered me a small percentage of Joni Mitchell's publishing, I wouldn't have had to write this book.

20

ow did another actor of comedy who worshipped by David's side in the Temple of the Second City venture an idea to David for a catalyst of laughter priorly unheard in comedy—and that manner would be amusement regarding God, Whose scintillating dry wit had been recognized only by a few but Whose temper was dreaded by most, for they assumed He hath not the disposition to enjoy the pokes of fun at Himself without showering the poker in excruciating wrath. Indeed, it was understandable how, by His own actions and rules, one might reach such a conclusion.

In such time and place, as in all other times and places, God was reckoned not suitable exchange at the water cooler unless you were president, pope, or had a television show early Sunday mornings on which you extolled to the populace of God's intention that vast sums of money not sit idly collecting compound interest when instead they could be to better use put in the pleasuring of God's alleged messenger on earth; and that earthly messenger shall then use such donations to spread further God's Good News, which was that God had chosen him as a messenger to live comfortably and well on their capital, in order that his camel pass through a needle's eye far more easily than he could into heaven.

To God, this was funny stuff, which explains why He did not cause the righteous freezing of funds, but for some reason the believing populace usually missed the joke and sent the cash. Nor did the populace perceive God's sense of humor at work in the everyday business of living—like rush hour, menopause, and Winnipeg. They believed that to see His humor would be as a blasphemy, with woe and rebuke to the blasphemer that you couldn't imagine, for they insisted that He preferred misery to mirth.

"David," stated his co-worshipper, "I really think you should do some bits about God and religion."

"Why?"

"Because it hasn't been done since Aimee Semple McPherson."

David had not fear of God's wrath, for, without punishment, he had already ignored God and otherwise spit in His face and abandoned His teachings and made a mockery of God and those who spoke in His name, like Amos and Ezekiel and Elijah and others who probably never got the kind of face time with Him that David had. And not only had David not been punished, he had thrived. That made David to lose a little respect for God, as God having spared the rod did spoilt this child; it was a tactical error that ipso facto undermined God's acumen in David's mind. Huzzah, David saw not the need for Him in the way that Martin didn't need Lewis (or was it Lewis who didn't need Martin?).

So of course David had not thought to think to bring God into the act as a silent Partner in the way that he preferred not to share the stage with children and dogs. Besides, it was one thing to diss the G-man for the benefit of your friends in seminary (which was to them the equivalent of dropping acid and *not* seeing God), and another to address an audience of many, among whom might be those to take offense at mentions of the Big Fella's idiosyncrasies and demand a vengeful rebuking that would include, but be not limited to, stoning, flaying, bankruptcy, and erectile dysfunction.

"You're right," David said. "It's perfect."

Thus did David, on stage at Second City, face his audience alone and intend a biblical oration without prearranging what to orate on. And so did he ask of the audience for biblical suggestions, and after a long pause the first of these came, "Douche bag," to which David explained that he preferred the Old Testament. Now they in the seats thought on this further and at last came a voice offering the name of the one who led his people in dusty circles for forty years.

Declared David promptly, "Moses had a wonderful rapport with God, whom I'm sure you'll all remember from last week's sermon."

And they in attendance offered him laughter, not stones, and he continued, and they laughed in liberation at hearing their fears and doubts and questions voiced out of the darkness. Oh, the taboo was broken, and his words were as welcome as the fingers of shiatsu masseuses upon the back knots of businessmen who need not shell out an extra twenty for a happy ending. True, the act may have been blasphemous but it had legs, and no rehearsal was necessary, as each night came a different shout from a different patron of a different Jonah or Jeremiah or Onan (a crowd favorite), each bringing the imagined sermons whose words flew to David's lips like marketing opportunities to Paris Hilton's agents. And soon the fame of David's sermons brought him attention from many sources, for his performances did not jump the shark.

21

This was proceeding as God had designed it, for He was not as they believed of Him, especially the they who believed that expressions of pleasure displeased Him—as do whole regions of His people living in proximity to oil reserves, as well as by Jewish women who shut their eyes during the act of intercourse so as to avoid witnessing the gratification of another, as well as by they who choose for their campfire harmonies "Taps."

He did not comprehend why so many of His people long ago had decided that they should hang garlic from their necks and cross themselves at the mere mention of frivolous laughter and witticisms about Him. Had not He given them Kato Kaelin?

Nor did He understand why they had continued to pass on the fictional narrative that He would reward despair and denial with ocean view suites and room service in the afterlife.

All right, yes, that was semantic dogshit. Of course He knew why they thought what they thought; He knows all whys, whether He likes them or not, especially when they call into question His opaque management style. It was because His people assumed that with life being so shitty and all that they had best keep their heads down and noses clean and call not too much attention to themselves by enjoying the few miserable years they had allotted to them in this stinking hellhole that He had created. Apparently, they had decided to believe that the more sorrowful they were on this earth, the more likely they were to be compensated with numberless enjoyments on the other side. There is, of course, a logic to that. Because when you work for a Boss who punishes His people throughout time in order to get back at one of their own for eating an apple that He Himself had put there and made delectably red, it's better than even money that He has the humor of a German nun.

God accepted how they had reached that conclusion with their free will, just as they had once brilliantly deduced that the sun revolves around the earth and that Zeus was his equal. To God, this was entertainment with a purpose, watching His people trial-and-error their way to the truth like testing to see how long a dog requires to shake the towel off his head. Oh, they get to the truth of things eventually, His people do, but eventually can seem to take too long, even if You're the One Who constructed the time-space continuum.

In truth, God had chosen to create joy and laughter for His people (no matter how they might disappoint Him, day after day, the scheming, thankless wretches), and indeed, His mysterious ways had been devised as the biggest joke of all, the one at which He had hoped for them to laugh aloud, "Ha, ha, ha, God, you're such a Pisser"; or even to exclaim to each other, "And God's like, 'Dude, rock on', and they'd be like, 'Omigod, I did not know that,' and He'd be like, 'Duh!'"

Alas, He realized, His way of demonstrating to them His intentions had been a little too ambiguous. They were such thick creatures sometimes, His people.

But now, at last, even with no grand therapeutic epiphany, He agreed that the time had come to be a little more out there and show them that, while He was still God Almighty and a force to be reckoned with, He was no sycophant-loving ogre. In fact, their fear and sniveling made Him contemptuous enough of them sometimes to contemplate instituting Plan B: another flood, and then starting over with a different, less pathetic breed—like the one He had read about in Nietzsche. Maybe this time He would choose a test group—the French, for they were the most expendable—then see how it went before going wide.

He was no quitter, though, and had chosen to stick with this breed of human, warts and all (created on the frivolous eighth day, after bloating), for, disappointing as they may be sometimes, these were still His people.

And now they needed to be less fearful of Him.

Yet here again, in revealing more of Himself, He had to maintain the fine balance that it had taken Him millennia to construct, one heartbreak and calamity at a time, in order not to favor either believers or atheists, the latter being particularly valuable to Him as His bellwether for how He was being perceived. Oh, how He loved them especially and did not want to lose them to the other side, for they feared not to take His name vainly and also were somewhat less likely to call out to him, except in times of peril and copulation. So He could not exactly shout to His people, "My bad on the whole comedy thing," for that would have made of everyone a believer—and that was something he could not abide. Maybe at one time that had seemed like a good idea. But in His growth, He had changed His Mind, because, as He'd learned, He gets to do whatever He goddamn well pleases.

So here now had come His Plan, which comprised of two parts: First, He created a man of various comedic entertainments and blessed him with a schlong the size of a grande bean-and-cheese burrito, for only such a man would possess the *cojones* to perform in drag for an audience of fifty-five million every Tuesday on national television.

And this was a good and cunning start to the Plan, for He knew that His people were like frogs and must be heated slowly, accommodated in increments, or they would leap from the boiling water.

Oh, too bad that He could not share this with them, as criminals sometimes betray their crimes with bragging. This was a more clever Plan by far than any since He hurtled that meteor to kick up dust that extincted His dinosaurs and cleared the land in advance of Adam and Eve—for gathered in front of their televisions His people were soon swept in jollity and laughed helplessly at the frolics of their beloved Uncle Miltie. And soon they accepted that men in dresses and lipstick were not to be burned at the stake as sacrifices to Him, which represented a great barrier fallen in his overall scheme to move them along toward Bertrand Russellism.

And now followed part two of the Plan, which came to pass when He placed on stage David to blaspheme without reprimand from Above.

"Joseph," for example, would come the suggestion, and then would David exclaim, "As you know, Joseph was the Bible's first homosexual. Yes, that's right. And I'm not referring to his coat of many colors—though Liberace would've swooned for it. No, the evidence is that Joseph managed to spurn the advances of his master's beautiful wife when she threw herself at him. So here we have a young man at the height of sexual potency and desire, and a naked, beautiful, horny girl of about eighteen who needed the big one right then and there. And she needed it from him. And he said no? That's just not possible. No straight guy I've ever met could've pulled that off. Now, if you think some young stud could resist because he was thinking about the kind of really bad, slow, horrible death that faced him if they'd gotten caught, you can forget it—'cause he would've forgotten it, too. No. The truth is, his master knew he could trust his servant alone with his wife, even if he couldn't trust his wife alone with his servant. And how'd he know that? Right. Hey, this was Egypt."

Hallelujah, the witnesses nightly at the Temple of the Second City, where the two-drink minimum had been applicable since 1957, could see David alone on the dais, beneath exposed wires and other assorted apparati—where falling lights or electrocution or Kristallnacht or any expression of God's catastrophes and malevolence could easily befall him. These were witnesses of intelligence, learned people, amateur historians, some of them, who were familiar with the revulsions that had laid low even righteous men like Job and Darwin and Ken Lay. So what would become someone who disses the Almighty intentionally? The deserving punishment could not be imagined. So at first they remained far from the seats down front, to avoid the hazard that they might become collateral damage once the retribution rained thickly on David.

And yet, on a nightly basis, as well as Sunday matinees, the sinful sermonizer remained unharmed as he requested ideas without aid of a shill, and riffed on (should the name be called out), for example, Shem, son of Noah—who was, God had claimed, a crummy slacker, reaching a hundred before begetting his first child, Arphaxad. No doubt this accounted for why he was kept alive another five centuries, for that's how long it would take to satisfy the compulsory begetting quota instituted for purposes of crash repopulation following His original genocide. Sadly, there were days Shem staggered home so dog-tired from the work of seeding women, some of them young enough to be his great-great-great-great-great-great-granddaughter (indeed, some of them *were* his great-great-great-great-great-great-granddaughters), that he cried out, "Oh, Lordy, give this bent and withered schvantz a breather."

These were the epochs before the Law was given to Moses, so Shem received not even Saturdays off from the occupation of re-creating His people. For Shem, it was nothing but fuck, fuck, fuck 24/7, all because the Lord Whom his father had agreed to do a favor for had gotten a little cranky one day.

Same for why Onan found himself on God's bad side.

The idiot had spilled his seed by his own hand, in soil where it could not grow. What a schmuck. Here he was, in the time of times for men's men, when it was a transgression for chicks not to swallow and guys got all the booty they wanted—and yet the dummy went and beat off like a fourteen-year-old with a *Delilah's Secret* catalogue. That's absolutely the kind of guy you do not want in the gene pool anyway, though you have to wonder about God if He takes Onan out for choking the chicken instead of doing his cute sister-in-law, but He lets Cain get all the poontang he wants for another couple hundred years after whacking his brother.

22

Thus or thereabouts did David riff on God's intriguing sense of humor, which was, as he pointed out, obviously all in the details. And thus was he not punished with any manner of persecution or suffering but in fact rewarded with triumph and acclaim when the patrons' word of mouth carried far and wide and announced him to be "a breath of fresh air in the stuffy room of Eisenhowerian homogeneity and post-assassination trauma that make life a living hell for those under the yoke of small-town bigots who run the big cities, and evil corporations that care more about capital than they do people." (Or words to that effect.)

Getting this memo were specific hordes of the country, and they read between the lines (for they understood not the lines themselves), and this was excellent for David, who was not a Machiavellian authority or a Lockheed director but rather the one to jab his finger in God's eye without visible punishment. And for that, his fame multiplied.

David's sermons became the dessert at Second City for which His people and their congregants had saved room and could not leave satisfied without. And they laughed and applauded at the blasphemies, and felt liberated by their profane laughter and applause, and asked of him that he rinse and repeat so that they might expunge further their bourgeoisness and come cleanly reborn to the experience in future visitings. But once and only once each night was enough, and they left desiring always more and coming back for more that was never enough.

And they respected him for his artistic choices, even when he was tanking.

Indeed, especially when he was tanking.

For they knew not what they did when they applauded.

For the will of God trumps everything, even bad material.

23

ow soon did the repute of Second City grow west to the Pacific Ocean and then north to David's former homeland on the social tundra, which was in the midst of a protracted identity crisis.

Now then did Second City fly to London, which is in a foreign land that was in the midst of a vast cultural exchange program with its former colonies, sending there young male musicians of long hair and sometimes dubious musical skills who wished to have been born African Mississipians. In exchange they received belatedly young, mostly Hebrew Americans of impious attitude who were demanded to gift to England's bewigged Lord High Chamberlain their written scripts of words to be spoken on stage. For this was an ancient land, which twice in its long history had sent its Hebrews packing on short notice, and it enjoyed a long and excellent tradition of censorship requiring preapproval of words spoken on stage in order to prevent the delicate ears of the stiff-lipped populace from hearing blasphemies against Queen or God, in that order.

Alas, they the performers of Second City had not the written scripts for scrutinous preapproval and thus could not obey the commandment to comply, which placed the performances in jeopardy of being banished from the kingdom and therefore the collection of such needed gate receipts as would avert pulling a runski on the hotel bills and fleeing for Heathrow before the bread rose.

Now then did David inscribe script words on a page. And at the time they seemed funny to him, and he intended to say them on stage, and then he got out there on stage, and then there went the script. And when unscripted profane words were uttered, the populace felt their ears tingle with pleasant wickedness, like the kind of agreeable ringing brought on by naughty naughty spanking that they and their Anglican brethren often preferred in advance of and during biblical knowing. And they the populace whose favorite laugh makers had come courtesy of the Morecambe and Wise Christmas Show did soften their stiff lips and express their amusement aloud without fear of national embarrassment on their teeth, which at this time resembled portions of the capital city yet awaiting repair lo these many years after the unfortunate blitz that God had prevented from going the way of Sodom and Gomorrah.

And it came quickly to pass that the Lord Chamberlain's man who had witnessed and heard the affront did report to the Lord Chamberlain, a man who was not much amused at hathing been flimflammed by the Americans. Thus did he proclaim that the Second City actors could arouse laughter no more on his soil, for he had taken their

And so David kept working, which indeed was His plan exactly. And it was working beautifully, as most of His plans do.

Then, two days before taping, the estate of Sholem Aleichem decided that none of Aleichem's actual words could be used in the play. Panicked, the producers asked me if I could make up a bunch of stuff that sounded "Aleichemesque." Being twenty-six, I said sure, and that's exactly what I did. The show went on as scheduled and was a smash success. I myself was nominated for an Emmy. *The New York Times* gave it a rave but noted: "Of course, how could Steinberg go wrong, given that all he had to do was use Aleichem's words?" Alas, I did not win the Emmy, probably because my main competition was Fellini's *The Clowns.* That talentless bastard.

American mischief personally and David's sermons most personally. Thus did he banish them all from the public stage on which they had offended the whole of Western civilization and primarily his vanity.

Oh, did such an uproar arise in the land at the proclamation when the newspapers saw fit to report the laughter of they who had felt their ears tingle and then lived to tell the tale. And tell they did, to their neighbors, with no loss of their previous righteousness—for this, too, was part of God's great plan for His multitudes to lighten up.

Now they of English descent who had not seen the first performance and who had not planned to see the second or third performance or any performance, despaired of having missed the only performance and sought to rebuke the Lord Chamberlain himself, who they agreed tended to take his title too literally. And they insisted that the edict be amended much as God Himself had once wielded a blue pencil to the longer list of commandments—deleting, for example, "Thou shalt not take unto thee a sheep for a wife," which was a load off for the Scottish but did little to increase their overall population.

Now then in the name of liberty and free expression and unclean amusement did the writer whose name was John Osborne lead a mob of villagers and artists to the edge of rhetoric overkill by expressing a range of angers looking both forward and back against the Lord Chamberlain and against the law and against the Lord God Himself. And Second City became to them a symbol of the shining city on the hill, for it required not stiff lips and an umbrella.

Oh, there was much anger, much outrage, much displeasure, much celebration at the anger and outrage and displeasure. Not since the golden calf showed up on Page Six and became what the ancient Hebrews used to call a "cause célèbre" had His people (chosen or not) so gloried in their ire. And this pleased God to witness how well pleased with themselves they were in the service of their own laughter. And then did the Lord Chamberlain nominate himself to receive the Maginot Award for redrawing his line in the sands of public estimation and allowing Second City to return to the stage without scripts or preapproval.

Thus, David spake his sermons to them, and there were other consequences in history (see: Decline and Fall).*

And thus did Second City remain for a time in this foreign land, where David made the acquaintance of a singer with aspirations, and her name was called Carly Simon, and not only were she and David acquainted but soon they knew each other well. She did not think him vain.†

---

* The *Star-Spangled Jack Show,* starring four members of Second City and three members of the English improv group The Establishment, was shut down by the authorities after the first performance when I would not submit my sermons to the Lord High Chancellor (since I didn't know what I was going to say until I actually said it). Then came the outcry, followed by the well-publicized reopening, which made the show the hottest ticket in London. Thus, once again, I had stepped in crap that turned to gold.

† When I left Second City and moved to New York, I lived in a building on First Avenue one floor above three sisters—Carly Simon, Joanna Simon, and Lucy Simon.

24

Now then came a blessed time for David Steinberg and for God, Who has as many blessed days as He cares to, for He is in charge of dishing out the blessings, though He is not a selfish God who Bogarts all the good blessings for Himself. In truth, He bestowed numerous blessings to David. David was of course to share them with the world, but knowing not of his crucial role in this mysterious Plan, he believed that the laughter he heard was for him and not because God had commanded it.*

---

*One symbol of my good fortune was my being asked by producer Ernie Pintoff to write a television play for an NBC show called *Experiments in Television*. The title: "This is Sholem Aleichem." I translated some of Aleichem's works from the Yiddish, compiling vignettes that highlighted several of the great author's characters. Everyone, including the cast led by Nancy Walker and Jack Gilford, loved the result.

25

od couldn't hold back a smile. For soon did *Time* declare that He was still dead. Good news for the Plan, yes, but not a very original line. They had probably cribbed the CliffsNotes of His beloved Nietzsche, whose wretchedness had reminded Him of Solomon's melancholy songs (downloaded to His iPod-inscribed "Ipod"). Badly was He dying to quip that such reports of His demise had been exaggerated.

So why did He not quippeth so? Surely, thou, the answer is already known:

To whom would He offer such a quip.

Billy Graham?

No, for that would be as preaching to the choir, which seemed to Him a waste of divine resources and less plausible than the *Da Vinci Code*. Who outside the choir, after all, would accept the testimony of someone with such vested interests in God's longevity? The examples are many and everywhere and eternal: they of His people who proclaim themselves to be His authorized franchisees and have only the check stubs and ranch houses as proof.

Perhaps, then, He should have chosen a nonbeliever for the sharing of His inside joke, which could then have reverberated and been dismissed not so readily.

Indeed, He had His eye on two nonbelievers, and their names were Eldridge Cleaver and Linda Lovelace, and their times would come eventually (as would Courtney Love's), but to no net gain in subscribers. And that is the rub. That is why he chose not a messenger now, for He is not a naked emperor. He perceives with a cold, clear eye what ordinary functioning people believe of they who claim to shoot shit with the Almighty. (What goes on in the afterlife stays in the afterlife, no matter what Lazarus says.) Throughout the populated millennia He had seen hordes of His correspondents turned into screaming shish kebabs at the auto-da-fé, because even those of His people who most devoutly testify intimacy with Him, and disdain belief in dinosaurs older than six thousand years, and praise His miracles past—like the raising to life or heaven of corpses—even they tend to look sideways and get a little squirrelly when Mrs. Gail Jones of Corpus Christi, Texas, says that God dropped in on her mah jongg group.

Know ye well that He had not the need to strut the honor of His excellent majesty on Oprah or reveal to Barbara Walters His preference as a tree. For the Lord God Almighty was gladly content to pretend refuge in doubts and anonymity, as this was the Plan, come hell or high water (with both of which He had had expertise). And from this roost He could monitor the reactions to His peoples'

American mischief personally and David's sermons most personally. Thus did he banish them all from the public stage on which they had offended the whole of Western civilization and primarily his vanity.

Oh, did such an uproar arise in the land at the proclamation when the newspapers saw fit to report the laughter of they who had felt their ears tingle and then lived to tell the tale. And tell they did, to their neighbors, with no loss of their previous righteousness—for this, too, was part of God's great plan for His multitudes to lighten up.

Now they of English descent who had not seen the first performance and who had not planned to see the second or third performance or any performance, despaired of having missed the only performance and sought to rebuke the Lord Chamberlain himself, who they agreed tended to take his title too literally. And they insisted that the edict be amended much as God Himself had once wielded a blue pencil to the longer list of commandments—deleting, for example, "Thou shalt not take unto thee a sheep for a wife," which was a load off for the Scottish but did little to increase their overall population.

Now then in the name of liberty and free expression and unclean amusement did the writer whose name was John Osborne lead a mob of villagers and artists to the edge of rhetoric overkill by expressing a range of angers looking both forward and back against the Lord Chamberlain and against the law and against the Lord God Himself. And Second City became to them a symbol of the shining city on the hill, for it required not stiff lips and an umbrella.

Oh, there was much anger, much outrage, much displeasure, much celebration at the anger and outrage and displeasure. Not since the golden calf showed up on Page Six and became what the ancient Hebrews used to call a "cause célèbre" had His people (chosen or not) so gloried in their ire. And this pleased God to witness how well pleased with themselves they were in the service of their own laughter. And then did the Lord Chamberlain nominate himself to receive the Maginot Award for redrawing his line in the sands of public estimation and allowing Second City to return to the stage without scripts or preapproval.

Thus, David spake his sermons to them, and there were other consequences in history (see: Decline and Fall).*

And thus did Second City remain for a time in this foreign land, where David made the acquaintance of a singer with aspirations, and her name was called Carly Simon, and not only were she and David acquainted but soon they knew each other well. She did not think him vain.†

---

* The *Star-Spangled Jack Show,* starring four members of Second City and three members of the English improv group The Establishment, was shut down by the authorities after the first performance when I would not submit my sermons to the Lord High Chancellor (since I didn't know what I was going to say until I actually said it). Then came the outcry, followed by the well-publicized reopening, which made the show the hottest ticket in London. Thus, once again, I had stepped in crap that turned to gold.

† When I left Second City and moved to New York, I lived in a building on First Avenue one floor above three sisters—Carly Simon, Joanna Simon, and Lucy Simon.

24

ow then came a blessed time for David Steinberg and for God, Who has as many blessed
days as He cares to, for He is in charge of dishing out the blessings, though He is not a selfish God who
Bogarts all the good blessings for Himself. In truth, He
bestowed numerous blessings to David. David was of
course to share them with the world, but knowing not of
his crucial role in this mysterious Plan, he believed that
the laughter he heard was for him and not because God
had commanded it.*

---

*One symbol of my good fortune was my being asked by producer
Ernie Pintoff to write a television play for an NBC show called *Experiments in Television*. The title: "This is Sholem Aleichem." I translated
some of Aleichem's works from the Yiddish, compiling vignettes that
highlighted several of the great author's characters. Everyone, including the cast led by Nancy Walker and Jack Gilford, loved the result.

And so David kept working, which indeed was His plan exactly. And it was working beautifully, as most of His plans do.

Then, two days before taping, the estate of Sholem Aleichem decided that none of Aleichem's actual words could be used in the play. Panicked, the producers asked me if I could make up a bunch of stuff that sounded "Aleichemesque." Being twenty-six, I said sure, and that's exactly what I did. The show went on as scheduled and was a smash success. I myself was nominated for an Emmy. *The New York Times* gave it a rave but noted: "Of course, how could Steinberg go wrong, given that all he had to do was use Aleichem's words?" Alas, I did not win the Emmy, probably because my main competition was Fellini's *The Clowns*. That talentless bastard.

25

❦

od couldn't hold back a smile. For soon did *Time* declare that He was still dead. Good news for the Plan, yes, but not a very original line. They had probably cribbed the CliffsNotes of His beloved Nietzsche, whose wretchedness had reminded Him of Solomon's melancholy songs (downloaded to His iPod-inscribed "Ipod"). Badly was He dying to quip that such reports of His demise had been exaggerated.

So why did He not quippeth so? Surely, thou, the answer is already known:

To whom would He offer such a quip.

Billy Graham?

No, for that would be as preaching to the choir, which seemed to Him a waste of divine resources and less plausible than the *Da Vinci Code*. Who outside the choir, after all, would accept the testimony of someone with such vested interests in God's longevity? The examples are many and everywhere and eternal: they of His people who proclaim themselves to be His authorized franchisees and have only the check stubs and ranch houses as proof.

Perhaps, then, He should have chosen a nonbeliever for the sharing of His inside joke, which could then have reverberated and been dismissed not so readily.

Indeed, He had His eye on two nonbelievers, and their names were Eldridge Cleaver and Linda Lovelace, and their times would come eventually (as would Courtney Love's), but to no net gain in subscribers. And that is the rub. That is why he chose not a messenger now, for He is not a naked emperor. He perceives with a cold, clear eye what ordinary functioning people believe of they who claim to shoot shit with the Almighty. (What goes on in the afterlife stays in the afterlife, no matter what Lazarus says.) Throughout the populated millennia He had seen hordes of His correspondents turned into screaming shish kebabs at the auto-da-fé, because even those of His people who most devoutly testify intimacy with Him, and disdain belief in dinosaurs older than six thousand years, and praise His miracles past—like the raising to life or heaven of corpses—even they tend to look sideways and get a little squirrelly when Mrs. Gail Jones of Corpus Christi, Texas, says that God dropped in on her mah jongg group.

Know ye well that He had not the need to strut the honor of His excellent majesty on Oprah or reveal to Barbara Walters His preference as a tree. For the Lord God Almighty was gladly content to pretend refuge in doubts and anonymity, as this was the Plan, come hell or high water (with both of which He had had expertise). And from this roost He could monitor the reactions to His peoples' growing deduction that He had laid down his terrible swift sword, donned love beads, grown out His hair, painted his winged chariots in psychedelic colors, and played lead guitar for Strawberry Alarm Clock.

And this was good, what He observed—though it meant enduring the assault of hearing and then returning unopened several billion fervent prayers that He reveal Himself to be the God that they had known and feared over the centuries; for in many of His people there is great comfort and benefit taken in the familiar, no matter its excruciation. (See: Clinton marriage.)

But in the end, He had come to know, His people were less likely to turn from Him and His ways, and more liable to continue residing in His house and not flee in rebellion, if they believed not that they would be beaten and scorched in hellfire for voicing the truth as they observed it. What they observed was that He seemed to have the soul of Edith Piaf but the comportment (now and then) of the Sex Pistols.

Oh, they longed to make Him aware of this personality tic, some of them did, for they believed that with such brutally honest communication and sharing and unburdening can there be achieved freedom, which brings closeness. And after counting to ten instead of giving Mel Gibson great powers over them, which was His first instinct, He became contented by their intentions. Which explains why He chose to show them that He hath not the thin skin of Dr. Laura.

Of course, revealing this new knowledge to them had to be done a little more subtly than the polka cover of "Smells Like Teen Spirit."

And this was the reason God continued to hide from David and would not declare and reunite with His young friend until the day came when He was goddamned good and ready, and that day was not yet.

26

~~✻~~

avid did not ask where God had gone, for David did not trouble where God had gone or whose company He was keeping now, for in their meets the Lord God Almighty had taken Himself way too seriously, and struck David as being somewhat less interesting and persuasive than a Pocket Fisherman infomercial.

Since then, David had matured and was working gainfully and getting laid with biblical regularity. And though he was inclined not to thank God for these blessings, he would not have minded if God texted him now and then, or left a short voicemail from time to time, just to check in and say hi—for olde time's sake.

But David did not ponder on this unreasonably in time, for he understood well that he himself and all of His people were as only humble grapes in the Host of hosts' vineyard. And in this world of His making (so theoretically He would have to understand, even if He didn't like it), sometimes relationships change and people change and it's no one's fault, really, when they grow apart. And if God had ever inquired in that mysterious way of His about the distance that He had noticed between them, David would have responded, "It's not about You, God, it's about me, but I hope we can always be friends."

Which was the truth—for indeed David had gone cold turkey on lying, except for the service of laughter.

And in this there was great irony, for now the multitudes in David's life had begun to lie every time they spoke, and they lied even about lying, and so was now the outcome the same as it has always been, with David destined always to be a vine apart from the cluster.

Such was exactly His plan, for He had the benefit of the long view.

27

⁊⁊ irst class on someone else's shekel did David journey to the land of Machu Picchu, a land of uncapitalized gods in a region as foreign as any Canadian province in which French is spoken (if you can call that French). And these were the days when Machu Picchu was not yet a land where the right people had stopped going, for as yet the right people had not made their virgin visits necessary to develop ennui. So here was David, a pioneer in Machu Picchu on assignment to smile for a camera in a commercial extolling Braniff Airlines, produced by Mr. and Mrs. Henry Nadlebaum of Potchemtuchas Springs, Florida.* And by showing the pleasures of alpaca, the commercial would do for international travel what Nuremberg did for rope.

---

* Their names have been changed to protect them from recognition. Somewhat surprisingly, given their profound incompetence, they never again worked in show business.

Oh, the elevated height of Machu Picchu above where His high tide wreaks damage to beach houses that are not covered by Allstate was greatly more than the multiples of *chai* pledged by the Moskowitzes on the holy days after their father passed away. And in that high altitude he was feeling poorly his fourth evening in the square of the town after a taxing day of smiling to the camera when now came David's name uttered by a dulcet female.

"Da-vid," came the dulcet utter.

And there was too much promise and pleasure and youth in this voice to be Mrs. Nadlebaum, so he turned toward the sound instead of blowing it off and pretending altitude-induced deafness in case she asked later why he did not her bidding. And now for what David saw did he believe that he had ascended to heaven.

For there was a young woman, and she had nineteen years then, and she had been blessed with a beauty for which men would volunteer to be butchered like anthrax-infected cattle if they had to, if only they could know her—that is, really, really know her, over and over again, deeply and gymnastically, with no moments necessary for recovery, followed by room service. Holy shit, hers was such a face that if it had been God's, there would yet remain no unbelievers among 97 percent of males and a goodly majority of females who, studies show, tend to more affirmatively select their sexual preference—and God knows, they would prefer her in a nanosecond. Hey, God can say what He likes, but He's only kidding Himself if He thinks this woman was made in His image. He should be so lucky.

And her name and face were soon to be recognized for

her contributions to the screen that would surpass David's work in the service of alpaca, which was a local product that grew on a beast closely related to the camel, allowing David to feel an instant visceral kinship. But that was not necessary to know on this night. All that was necessary to know on this night was that this woman was familiar to a friend of David, and they had priorly met once near to home, and she remembered his name, and she had called to him and perhaps wanted to know him as perhaps she had heard that he had many times and in many locations and imaginative poses known her singing acquaintance; and perhaps she had heard further in detail how he had managed to pour out his spirit into the singer through his body in hers and had caused her to experience such glory as at the moment of God's throwing the switch on the Big Bang.

Oh, how David prayed that this woman had been apprised of such news of his prowess.

But alas, she had not—wait, until that very instant(!), when suddenly the false memory appeared in her mind, and it dwelled in her attention of him. (God could be such a good friend sometimes.) Oh, but unless she made the first move, there would be no knowing tonight, no switches, no spirit, no face of God—for David had been fortunate in the sack and thus had not needed to acquire the knowledge of first-move making.

The odds, however, were with him, for on this night he and she were far from home; and free (and has it yet been mentioned that she was nineteen?); and she was pictur-esque—oh my God; and she was learned; and she floated in the air as she was seated on a smile at a café with Henry

Yokamura, who said to David, "Hey, meshuggah, hert zikh mit di zakhn? Mit a shiksa meg men lign," for Yokamura had visited Canaan's kibbutzim and acquired lingo.*

David felt more blessed than Adam before the fall but desired to show it not (see: junior high school), and so asked of Henry what it was that they over there were masticating, they being the short men of foreign appearance against the wall in strange hats and tans and coats of many colors.

Now then did Henry show his pleasure, for it had come to happen only in the moments before David's passing that another son of Judah (in Peru on a fellowship, of course) had entrusted to Henry for keeping a bag. And in this bag that Henry lifted onto the table was the answer to David's question. And the answer was the leaves and stems of a plant that the local heathens practiced to chew in place of throwing back a double shot mocha latte, though the heathens chewed not to propel them into a day at the office but through the finding of more plants to chew, which in this region seemed as logical a profession as any.

"Coca leaves," did Henry answer. "You wanna try?"

David replied not, his tongue suffering like the rest of him under a wicked hex cast by the actress. He had become very sorry of changing the subject in the first place instead of just saying hi to her without making such a big deal about maybe looking like he might want to fuck her brains out, as now he had talked himself into a situation and could not deduce what she would expect of him—to chew or not to

---

* This translates roughly to: "Wassup? You might get lucky tonight with this babe."

chew? Which of these was cooler, hipper, sexier? Such was the essential question, and he knew not the answer, for his mind had been stolen by desire. But yet at that moment, under pressure to speak, his mouth widened and he spoke without his own consent in horrifying confusion. And the words he spoke his own ears recognized not, for he was spaking in Christian tongues.

Said David, "Behold, my master wotteth not what is with me in the house, and he hath committed all that he hath to my hand. There is none greater in this house than I; neither hath he kept back any thing from me. How then can I do this great wickedness, and sin against God?"

"Hey, suit yourself," said Yokamura.

And on did David continue channeling King James, knowing not the meaning nor context nor punctuation of what passed his lips: "Therefore thou art inexcusable, O man, whosoever thou art that judgest: for wherein thou judgest another, thou condemnest thyself; for thou that judgest doest the same things."

"As if," said Yokamura, who now pondered in silence his further words learned from his native Sweden, before socialism kicked in and made girlie-men of former Vikings: "Behold thou art called a Jew, and restest in the law, and makest thy boast of God, and knowest his will, and approvest the things that are more excellent, being instructed out of the law."

And this was a proper response, and now came David's to it: "And shall not uncircumcision which is by nature, if it fulfil [*sic*] the law, judge thee, who by the letter and circumcision dost transgress the law? For he is not a Jew, which is one outwardly; neither is that circumcision, which is outward in the flesh: But he is a Jew, which is one inwardly; and circumcision is that of the heart, in the spirit, and not in the letter; whose praise is not of men, but of God. Hallelujah." And touché.

"Yeah, I see where you're coming from," said Yokamura. "But don't worry. You don't have to recompense me."

And thus was it settled as that, for his was a most convincing argument, and thus did David take from the bag and place into his mouth two leaves and begin their mastication while becoming enslaved by the eyes of this woman, knowing not that she would be unimpressed by such careless disregard for his health.

But in this moment, David chewed and grimaced at the taste and chewed harder, and she watched, and soon his manhood became abnormally aroused, as additional blood and other body fluids diverted from assorted regions and continued to surge that direction, stretching the member to lengths and widths worthy of an NBA star in a Colorado hotel but leaving too little nourishment for the remaining functions, including conscience (see: NBA star in a Colorado hotel).

Now she could not avoid noticing how very, very much she meant to him. Said David to her with no control of his tongue, for he was as no more than the dummy to his ventriloquist johnson, "I pray thee, let me come in unto thee," and she said to the dummy, for she had vast experience with this line of communication, "What will thou givest me, that thou mayest come in unto me?" and he said, "What I have to give thee should be incredibly apparent to thine eyes," and she said, "Believe me, it is," for it seemed in its growth that another guest had joined them at the table.

And now David in appreciation of begging as foreplay replied "Good," and she said, "How do I put this? I have been presented such ample offerings before," to which David noted that he believed he could hear playing softly in the clouds "Theme From a Summer Place," the Percy Faith instrumental version, which he accepted as a sign that he was ordained to score. As so it seemed.

Then did her eyes widen, and then did she speak in a voice of alarm, "I think you have Bell's Palsy."

Say what?

Verily had the chewing side of his cheek fallen out of symmetry, causing his appearance to recall for the actress *Guernica*, which she had viewed in person during her junior year abroad, where she was pinched and propositioned mercilessly by Catholic men of several nationalities.

"Fuck it," said David. "If I don't come in unto thee right now—"

"And oh my God, you're green," she uttered, rubbing her finger to his cubist face, which had turned the color of prescription myrrh.

Alas, the fever of desire had been broken by his grotesqueness, and she was now impervious to his entreaties and offerings. He tried, Lord knows, but "Please, please, please—I'll put a bag over my head" had lost its charms to work him into her jeans.

No, there would be no coming into anyone that night, except for David's knowing himself in a marathon of self-knowing—as there was something in the leaf that prevented blessed, welcome conclusion; and throughout till dawn did David wail and lament like a virgin girdled with sackcloth for the husband of her youth, which was a representation that appeared in his mind without context or explanation or power to assuage, for the mother of all hard-ons had been let go to waste. A *shonda*.

"Apparently," saith Yokamura, "you're supposed to chew the stems, not the leaves."

And this may not have been part of His original plan. God had not yet decided and would sort it out in the morning, after He stopped laughing. Apparently, even when he wasn't trying, David still made God laugh—though for laughing at David's expense instead of *with* him, God assigned Himself as penitence a dozen Hail Marys and five Our Fathers, which began, "Myself, who am in heaven, hallowed be My name."*

---

* I was in Peru shooting a promotional film for Braniff Airlines called *The Next Place*. Candice Bergen was in Peru shooting a layout for *Vogue*. She was a friend of Mary Ellen Mark, my then girlfriend who, no thanks to me, became one of the best photographers in the world. To this day, Ms. Bergen insists that we have never met—and certainly not in Peru. She may be right.

28

~~~

Once in the land there was a television show unlike other television shows that were like it (though not only because the Electric Prunes once appeared). It was a show airing on the Tiffany network and seen by His multitudes on the evening of the gentile Sabbath, but witnessed by fewer of His multitudes than the show witnessed immediately before it; for though this show also purveyed a variety of entertainers and entertainments, the really big shoe that came first was enjoyed by grandmothers and their children and their children's children, as there was a little something for everybody, including those who derive pleasure from Italian men in hats spinning plates to accordion music. Meanwhile, on this later show, grandmothers did not get the joke—and those who did, did not always like the joke they were getting. And of their children who got the joke, few of them liked being the punch line. Which basically left just the children's children as viewing congregants.

So that was why the show was a miracle victory of popularity but not as large a victory as the earlier show, for it had lost at least one generation of viewers, which was in fact the whole point of the show. Thus was it a show unlike, for such had not before been sought and achieved. (And this also explains the Electric Prunes.)

And the show was called for two brothers born to the punishing name Smothers, who enjoyed each other as well as did Cain and Abel and in appearance looked like the hired amusement at Shiva Pincus's bat mitzvah in 1959. Yet they offered much renegade humor directly to His younger multitudes and a haven to other entertainers of their same mind who also provided humor about a war that they did not like, and about a president they did not like, and about words that they did not like being not able to utter at will, and about thoughts that they did not like leaving unsaid—which were indeed all their thoughts. For theirs were the thoughts of God, they insisted, and all the rest that were the thoughts of others were absolute wickedness. And as yet, God had not disabused them of that notion, for He had just finished *Madame Bovary* and was busy reevaluating His penalties for romanticism, certitude, and youthful passion.

And now then did one of those other entertainers of like humor and thoughts and words become David, who caused to laugh the brothers Smothers with his riff on liberation theology.

David, as you recall, had had prior experience with such imprisoning decrees of muteness in a foreign land, and had come aware that if a foreign land which enjoyed not this land's 200-year statute of unshackled blather could cave, then the colonies were theirs for the defiance.

And so, using David as point man, did the Smothers resolve to break the yoke of restriction by pretending that they had not been tasked with providing in advance to the Tiffany network their entertaining words and deeds.*

And thus did David declare with a smile and smirk to thirty million of His middle-finger-raising young multitudes that his own ancient brother Jonah had been cast into the sea as whale bait by gentiles of a certain acronymic heritage called WASP. O, such was a Tiffany-unapproved declaration.†

Behold, there now rained wrath—terrible, though of a different brand of terrible from His really terrible wrath—as indeed was the yoke yet on them still. For this was in the epoch between Demi's and Ashton's births, and in such years WASPs were yet pleased and caring of their country clubs and Pilgrim ancestors and DAR lineage, and so they disgruntled aloud David's slander, and truly did they have the scratch and coin and smack and Rolodexes to turn the Tiffany network into Kmart's housewares department by tomorrow noon if the suits did not immediately heed their moans.

---

* The week after my first sermon on *The Smothers Brothers Show,* Tom Smothers guided me down a hallway and into a room that was piled almost ceiling high with mail. I asked what I was seeing. Tom explained that, according to Perry Lafferty, head of the network, "It's the most amount of negative mail CBS has ever gotten for anything that's ever been on the air." Needless to say, I drove home on a cloud.

† Following my first appearance, CBS had told the Smothers Brothers that "the comedian" was welcome to appear on the show again but that I couldn't do another sermon. So on my next appearance, I performed my soon-to-be-famous psychiatrist character (stolen from Groucho), which went so well with the audience that Tom said to me through a Cheshire grin, "You wanna do Jonah?"

Now then and quickly did the brothers Smothers find that they had not their druthers, as they and their fellows were canned by the suits for whom the euthanizing of a top-twenty show that congregated their all-important 18–34 demo was less pleasurable than donning in nakedness a codpiece from the Lorene Bobbitt Collection. But their duty was clear, as they could not stomach their FCC license becoming ass wipes.

Lo, this canning was to David and the Smothers and their others the surprise and shock of the century (not to be bettered until Reagan sent the air traffic controllers packing), for they, alas, had believed in righteousness as an impervious shield.*

Apparently, they had not been paying attention.†

And soon did this come to pass, that these events proved fortunate for David (as all things did, thank God), and somewhat less fortunate for the Smothers, who now had to pick grapes for a living.‡

---

* The Smothers Brothers seemed to harbor no bitterness toward me after I'd been responsible for having them thrown off the air, nor did Tom Smothers seem to mind that I had begun dating his secretary/ girlfriend, Judy Marcioni, who later appears in the narrative playing the role of Mrs. David Steinberg.

† A year after throwing the Smothers Brothers off the air, CBS gave me my own TV show. Not wanting to lose it prematurely, I naturally did not perform any sermons.

‡ Four years after their show went off the air, the brothers Smothers won a million dollars from CBS in a lawsuit by playing the sermons in the courtroom for a laughing jury. (Those were the days when jurors had wit, intelligence, and taste.) The proceeds were used to help found a winery that makes vintages every bit as good as their act is, which plays to sold-out houses in Vegas, with the sixty-nine-year-old brothers still arguing over who Mom liked best.

29

Tempus fugit. So had He decreed long ago (though it seemed not so very long, considering). And now then in time, though not too long now in time that has fugited, did David reach the culmination of his impulsive goal and stand up alone on a small stage as a simple man of humor, without props or makeup, being paid to elicit amusement in they who had been induced by the Great Satan of perpetual hipness to take a seat on its cutting edge at small tables without room for their elbows as they swallowed a minimum of two usuriously priced liquids that kept the club afloat financially.

And the name of the club that was no bigger than from here to there but which was of renown for its ahead-of-tempus entertainments was the Bitter End—a name of intended rich irony (see: Chamberlain, Munich, and "Peace in our time"); and this was in a southern region of a city where David had come for the purpose of knowing that if he was capable of making it there, he would then be knowing that he was capable of making it anywhere. And this region was called Greenwich Village, birthplace of *Queer Eye*. And in these days there were many Birkenstocks but no soccer moms.

For one week was David to occupy the stage preceding in paid entertainment a troubadour of imagination and wit called by his biblical name Tom Paxton, whose music was to folk songs what Tootsie Rolls are to candy. Before he brought them forth to sweeten the night came David, whose performance that first show was to humor what leaf blowers are to serenity—for this engagement had been one of those fluke things arranged by the Almighty without consultation.

Apparently, He was in a divine hurry for David to get on with it already. So David had not previously suffered crucial rites of comedy passage in the Catskills nor any out-of-town hellhole where he could ditch the sermons and see what else worked and what didn't without making an ass of himself in front of local Noël Cowards inclined to shout bon mots like "Ya jerky bastard, ya, get off the fucking stage" at comedic practitioners whose work compelled in such pitiless hearts the desire to TiVo™ past the crap.

Though this was not precisely what they shouted at David.

No, to David on this night they spoke in heckling discourtesy, "Honey, you're no Shecky Greene." For on this Wednesday night in the slow summer season had the Grey Line chariot deposited sightseers of a certain age beyond hipness (though yet inquisitive of its current form) who wished him by nature into the Valley of Death. So when David replied "Thou art no Perle Mesta" they did stand with a huff to depart in angry protest and disgust of updated mores.

Now there sat in the club with its sudden surfeits of elbow room a mere six people—and at them did David experience the reaction of Ishmael upon learning that Mom was not Jewish. Indeed, David showed not joy and gratitude at their remaining presence, as those of His people with reasonable breeding might assume, but instead contempt for their bad taste in being there altogether.* And two of the remaining six answered to the names Sidney Poitier and Dyan Carroll, and they were approving of his humor that included a snark regarding a certain Nixon whose face, observed David, appeared to be in truth a misplaced foot. Despite, laughter was not loud, nor drinks consumed in abundance, and management wanted him gone ASAP.

And thus came swiftly the last night of David's engagement, and when he stepped from the underground railway onto the public thoroughfare with an uncertainty of the future that was as deep as Kim Cattrall's jar of Astroglide, he saw multitudes awaiting. For what, he knew not, and so believed that they had appeared to pay witness to the one named Richard Pryor at the Congregation A Go Go, located in near biblical proximity to this Bitter End, which was the metaphor that David mused he had arrived at, his prospects snuffed like Egypt's GDP after that massive free-labor exodus.

---

* Usually what keeps a comedian showing up onstage when he's bombing is self-confidence—believing that the audience will someday catch up. In my case, it was Helga and Monique, two waitresses at the Bitter End whom I would belatedly like to thank.

Indeed, David was making appropriate plans to self-medicate after the show, and maybe catch the Mike Curb Congregation at the Copa, when hallelujah did he grasp with surprise that the waiting multitudes had come to witness not Brother Pryor but David Steinberg.

Hallelujah, he had been that morning sanctified in the holy *New York Times* by a scribe answering to Dan Sullivan, one of the four remaining to the bitter end in the Bitter End not named Poitier or Carroll. *Hmmm*, thought David as he read the notice at the bar and remembered the night previous, *this man Sullivan must either have uttered untruths in print or confined his laughter better than Nevada contains nuclear waste*, for David could recall seeing none appearing to enjoy himself sufficiently to engrave that the man speaking humor onstage was "a cross between Woody Allen and Lenny Bruce."*

But these had been the words of Sullivan. And their effect was swift and mighty. For that morning had the whole of the tristate region received on their doorsteps a complimentary copy of the *Times*, courtesy of the Almighty, so that His influential tastemaking Northeastern multitudes could obey the favorable notices and identify now the name David Steinberg and know further that they were commanded to come see him and laugh

---

* When they begin their careers, most comedians imitate the style of other comedians they admire. My predominant influences were Woody Allen and Lenny Bruce, but I did not believe that this form of flattery was so transparent until I read Dan Sullivan's review, calling me "a combination" of the two. I felt shamed and embarrassed—until that night when I saw the line stretching around the block outside the club. And then I wondered what else I could steal.

and spread his fame or risk exile from the influential taste-making conversation, which to Northeastern multitudes is to be wished less devoutly than finding your name in Heidi Fleiss's logbook.

And so they came, the multitudes did.

And so did they keep coming and spreading David's fame.

And then did David change locales, again and again. And always did the adajcent multitudes find him again and again—indeed, they were waiting when he got there.

Yea, this was as He desired it, which we accept because it happened thus, though it is as otherwise inexplicable as Vanna White.

30

~※~

nd a son had been born to parents skilled at
making doctors and lawyers, and this was good,
thank God, and they were well pleased with
their seven professional children, knock wood. But the
boy's father had once in his frivolous youth worn a belt of
borscht while dancing on soft shoes, and he mused with
contentment on those days past before his going into the
family tchotchke business, and he now enjoyed to have his
last child (!!!, declareth his wife) make a decent and honorable living in the arts, God willing, and so he had planned
bestowment of the Christian name Clark—until the child's
face emerged from the womb. And then the old father who
was no dummy recognized an Irving when he saw one.

And Irving did not disappoint his destiny, for he grew
to become what all Irvings are destined to become, and as
a macher agent he had a big-time client roster, and on that
roster was David—David Steinberg, he now called him-

self professionally, for no one bestowed at birth with John Smith had ever been paid for laughs.*

And now came the moment when Irving insisteth to David that the timing had arrived suitable for David to drink deeply and profitably from the Holy Grail of comedy, and that David accept the court summons from Pope Johnny Carson, who in his anointing hands held the power to bestow career blessings that pay off as surely as Ave Maria Mutual Funds. This was what Irving knew in instinct, for though the name of David had achieved recognition, Irving yet saw the young man's career as a menstruous virgin among steamy divorcées skilled at darting their tongues deliciously in the ear of New York—an argument to which David observed that perhaps Irving had

---

* Back in the day, it was considered career suicide for Jewish entertainers to use their real names. Hence, Joey Gottlieb became a Bishop, Allan Schmididowitz or whatever became a King, Allen Stewart Koenigsberg became Woody Allen, Leonard Alfred Schneider became Lenny Bruce, Erich Weiss became Houdini, Michael Peschkowsky became Mike Nichols, Ivo Levy became Yves Montand, etc. And no wonder. Conventional wisdom was that paying customers either wouldn't come to see or not take seriously anyone with an obvious Jewish name. So it was a big deal that I, David Steinberg, refused to become Brick Powers. Really, when I appeared at the Aladdin in Vegas with Frankie Valli, some people looking at the marquee thought he was performing with his accountant. When CBS gave me my own show (creatively titled *The David Steinberg Show*), network executives Freddy Silverman and Irwin Siegelstein were nervous that such a Jewish name would tarnish the network's reputation and tank the ratings. So why didn't I go along with the trend and change my name? Because if I had, then how could my second-grade teacher, Miss Krog, who'd predicted daily that I'd amount to a big fat nothing, know that it was me?

been inhaling too deeply and long from the agent's compulsory sack of bullshit.

Even so, David perceived the advisability and assembled for solo stage presentation his ten best minutes. O, they were not an ordinary ten minutes of ordinary "I just flew in from the coast and my arms are really tired" material. But they were a very good, if unusual, ten minutes about which he felt confident of a kill, for he had denied himself pleasure this week, as he believed that his legs ought to be fresh for the standing.

Thus did David and Irving await in the studio's room of green for Mr. Carson to summon him into the audience and camera and rub the anointing oils of his own amusement into David, for J.C.'s enjoyment was America's laugh track, gesturing acceptance of a humor worthy to please His multitudes across the fruited plain. O, but woe to comedians who inspired not this man's noticeable pleasure, for many had been the moment already in this his first decade of reigning when the camera located this host of all hosts appearing bummed by the wasting loss of unfunniness—moments of his show gone forever and never to be redeemed—and soon did they find themselves hosting karaoke Saturdays at the Trenton Ramada, for there is no affirmative action in comedy.

And on did David and Irving continue to wait in the room of green among delicious cold cuts and crudités as the show advanced, and guests were called out by ones and twos—James Bond, Rudolf Nureyev, Joe Namath, Robert Redford, Leonid Brezhnev, Ali McGraw, Thor Heyerdahl, Tricia Nixon, Sirhan Sirhan, Abraham Zapruder. David was written in stone to appear the last and the most funny, and he and Irving viewed on a private screen the others sing and dance and amuse Mr. Carson with their wit and talent. But never came David's name from Mr. Carson's lips, nor the parting of curtains for him. What came after ninety minutes was the test pattern and a commandment from a man recompensed for flicking lint from Mr. Carson's sport coat that David return a night hence.

Irving was pressed under the disappointment of rescheduling as a Brad-Angelina red carpet is crushed under entourages. But David saw in this a blessing and indeed rejoiced at not following Saigon police chief Nguyen Ngoc Loan's point-blank marksmanship exhibition, for such an act always brought down the house and laughs would be few in its wake.

Now then did David return again the next night to his seat in the room of green among others commanded also to appear for Mr. Carson, and then all that night did he and Irving wave goodbye to Henry Kissinger and Dennis Hopper (sans Peter Fonda) and Hugh Hefner and Spiro Agnew and Charles Manson and two Bond girls and Abbie Hoffman as each was summoned to the stage, and again did David's name not befall the host of hosts' lips.

And now again was David commanded to appear a third night, and in procession on that third night did Mario Puzo and Jean-Louis Trintignant and Glen Campbell and Bobby Fischer and Dmitri Tiomkin and Prince Sihanouk and Timothy Leary and James Earl Ray fill Mr. Carson and his multitudes with joy and wonder and pleasure, and steal David's appointment; and oy, did Irving let someone have it before receiving declaration that the fourth night would be different than all other nights, for on the fourth night David would be delivered from the room of green before all other guests.

Hmmm, though, thought David, who now began to suspect God's hand in the three disappointments which he did not understand but did not mind. Though he did pain with balls of blue that the week of denied pleasure had now reached ten nights, and he resolved that it would not reach eleven. And thanks to a Suzi on Johnny's staff, it did not.

Thus did the fourth night begin in the room of green, with David's legs a little less strong as he and Irving observed Andy Warhol and Simon sans Garfunkel and Neil Armstrong and Peg Leg Bates and Mary Jo Kopechne benefit from their face-time with Mr. Carson. And when appeared the surprise guest Chou en-Lai to share intimate memories of Mao and the Great Leader's own side-splitting recipe for kung pao enemies of the state ("Frist you sprit one side . . . "), David felt kinship with the forgotten Hananiah, born unwanted to Shelemiah, as well as Hanun, dim-witted sixth son of Zalaph, if not also Meshugganah, bastard child of Lindsay Lohan.

Then came the following night and another pageant of guests—William Westmoreland, Victor Borge, Berry Gordy, Papa Doc, Baby Doc, three Dionne quintuplets, the New York archdiocese, everyone who was at Woodstock, everyone who claimed they were at Woodstock, and Red Buttons. Alack, not David.

For forty nights this young man of jest was invited to return with the producer's ruby-lipped promises of moments in the national psyche. Yet he sat uncalled-upon, nibbling potato salad from the *traife* buffet—though so it shouldn't be a total waste, David had been padding his

Rolodex in the hours before the others claimed his spot in the zeitgeist ("Schmooze, boychik, schmooze," Irving had insisteth). And now was David beginning to suffer some loss of confidence in the acumen of his theatrical representative.

"What the fuck?" he inquired of Irving.

"What the fuck, what the fuck?" Irving cried out in return, for he, like many of his brethren, was wont to answer questions with questions.

"I'm just saying," said David.

"What're you saying?"

"I'm just saying, I'm just saying. It's a saying."

"You're just saying that you're just saying that you don't appreciate how much I'm protecting you," saith Irving. "I am. Believe me. I'm protecting you. That's what I do. I'm your agent. Agents protect."

"Don't get me wrong, Irving. It's nice getting to watch the show without staying up till one in the morning. But it's been two months of this. I feel like Tonya Harding crashing a *Disney on Ice* audition."

"They will not bump you again," declareth Irving. "Guaranteed. Tomorrow night, you're on for sure."

"They say that every night."

"Yeah but tomorrow's the real deal."

"How do you know?

"How do I know? How do I know, how do I know? I know because tomorrow night the only other guest is Tony Bennett, and the only thing he knows how to do is sing. You talk to him, he makes Elmer Fudd sound like William F. Buckley. The man has a voice from God, but he can't ask directions without the cop falling asleep. You'll see, he'll come out, he'll do a song, he'll sit down next to Johnny, he'll say hi, Johnny'll say how ya doin', he'll say great, just great, I'm in town at the Copa, Johnny'll say great, that's great, and then they'll look at each other and Johnny'll say, *tokka,* you look good, and Tony'll say you look good too, *kanehora,* and Johnny'll say how's it goin', and he'll say it's goin' great, thanks for asking, how's it goin' for you, and Johnny'll say not too bad and ask if anything's new, and Tony'll say no, not really, and Johnny'll make that funny face he makes when he's got a stiff out there, then go to commercial even if there isn't one scheduled, and that'll be that. Next thing you know, you'll be out on the stage, and Johnny'll be laughing, and I'll be beating off offers for you with a machete."

"A machete?"

"You just make sure you're ready, boychik. I'm your agent. I protect you."

And so came the forty-first night. And David brought to the room of green with him a carved tablet of his material in the knowing that after Mr. Bennett was called forth he would for a while be alone, uncounting Irving, in need to rehearse himself the dialogue unused now for many nights of a young man in mirthful banter with the Lord God Almighty. Such was the nature of the comedy of his act, which was not the act of a comedian but of a former performing congregant at the Temple of the Second City. Not yet had David acquired the material of a comedian. (This, in the view of God—He who watched with amusement from on High, eager to hear how He came off as David's second Banana—indicated an ironic dearth of effort on the part of a certain young man with ambitions actually to earn his living as a comedian. It seemed in His humble judgment to be less effort, even, than that put into composing the *Vagina Monologues*.)

In the standard hanging around before performance, David found Mr. Tony Bennett to be an agreeable companion, notwithstanding his green-table buffet scarfing of prosciutto and Siciliano spezzatino with porchetta chased by pigs' feet brine—delicacies brought especially for his pleasure by the producers from a hog farmer upstate in, o kosher irony, Beth El.

"Dig in, kid," he offered *con gusto* to David, who at the spectacle of the smorgasbord of *traife* wondered that he had dropped acid and stumbled onto Porkfest '69. Suddenly did he feel now a keen affection for even that abomination gefilte fish, and in trying to sail his mind far elsewhere and keep down yesterday's breakfast he began in all purity—as others for the same purpose might dwell on thoughts of Willie Mays—to hum Don Corleone's love theme.

But this quiet music, mistaken as a diss on olive oil heritage, was not esteemed by the man born Benedetto, who gazed now on David as a mohel sizes up his target or Winona Ryder the Prada inventory at Saks. It was a look that said not that David Steinberg sleeps with the fishes so much as David Steinberg Dances with the Stars. It was a look that seemed to say Yanni.

Now and not an eon too soon sounded the clarion for the singer of singers to materialize from the room of green and sing and thence to talk small with the host of hosts. Such was the indication for David to rise and prepare himself to make mirth for millions.

By the minutes of the clock, there were yet sixty

remaining in the program, and this was good, and this portended well, as Irving had so foretold. And the mortal who was God's favorite crooner completed his song and was motioned by the host to dwell on the couch for the deadly dull chatter that would soon beget David's summons.

Thus did David arise from his seat in preparation—just as began the vengeful wrath of Bennett, who David could see would not permit the little *halachic* putz that had slurred his birthright to succeed him onto the dais. O signs and wonders did Tony Bennett now convert, truly and nakedly before the eyes of America's national television, into Noël Coward, Bennett Cerf, Oscar Levant, John Kenneth Galbraith, Burt Reynolds, and *Bartlett's Quotations*, offering tales of wit, humor, erudition, and street cred that bid a speedy riddance of the host's plans to swap him on the couch. Hilarity ensued. Never had a guest so undone all the afflicted of their cares and woes since Mr. Blackwell dined alone at the White House.

And so in the six and sixtieth minute of the program did David now recognize with misery and certainty that the host had fallen in hopeless thrall to the fascination of the singer, and that his own prospect now appeared as bleak as the dysplastic three-legged Pomeranian's at Westminster.

Not for the first time, nor the last, did David recall freezing God out like the drunk fat girl at a party who wants to put her underpants on your head (with her in them). Believing that God must be sorely displeased with him, he anyway lifted his eyes to the heavens and wondered aloud whether he ought better to take that titty inspector job at airport security for which Issac Mizrahi had recommended him. But Irving would hear none of it, for Irving had had it up to here already with the forty days and nights of scorning his client, and so he lashed with tongue a nearby producer within a millicubit of his life.

David overheard his representative lashing thusly: "Listen, dickhead, do you know who my client is?"

"David Steinberg."

"No, not David Steinberg. David *Fucking* Steinberg. You understand the distinction?"

"Uh, no."

"Pissant," explained Irving, "David Fucking Steinberg isn't just any new stand-up piece-of-dreck comic. He's the hottest fucking comic in the business. You know it, I know it, everyone knows it—and you're treating him like my man Tupac pushing crack on the *700 Club*. I won't have it. I won't, I won't, I won't!!! And let me tell you something else, you miserable bone-smoking, fart-sucking gooch . . ."

The unpleasantries continued their spewment from the maw of Irving with a fury like that of Kate Moss when the coke drawer is snorted bare. For long minutes stretched Irving's conniption, and neither David Steinberg nor David Fucking Steinberg could hear the response of the lashed producer, but there was fury still residing in the face and voice of the artist's representative upon returning to his client's side. Came his words: "Get your coat on, David. We're outta here."

Though seasickened by confusion, David obeyed as he was instructed, for it was a glacial night in the city of New York. And as they made ready, all snugly and warm in their coats, to egress onto the streets of ice and loneliness, Irving did stop with suddenness and angle his (good) ear to the stage, from where was now heard the singer Bennett commencing "I Left My Heart in San Francisco." Said Irving: "Hold on, boychik, I love this song," and Irving did now forget about David and, evincing the stiff contentment of Father Shanley unchaperoned at preschool recess, enjoy the singer through the green monitor.

David reflected now on his ancient brother Job, who had suffered, yes, but not like this, for this was show-business suffering, and surely there was no suffering like show suffering, like no suffering he kneweth. Consider, what was the loss of earthly fortune and the slaughter of your offspring and the torching of your house compared with such a terrible thwarting of stage ambition as this? O, the agony. O, the torture. O, the excruciation of which Molly Ringwald would grasp an appreciation. For this in action was the cosmic flow chart on which celebrity lives are more precious. So saith the tabloids, they who identify the mahatma of fame (see: Greyhound station, Hollywood and Vine).

Now then did David desire enough Manischewitz to blow a good .10 on Officer McDougal's breathalyzer. Hark, though, this was not now necessary, for when the singer at last retrieved his heart in San Francisco, Irving declared with the smirk of a lobbyist in a room of Republican legislators that they were a shoo-in on the night following, for he had given to the lashed producer orchestra seats for the Jackson Family picnic at Bellevue, nineteenth floor north. "I'd promised Steven Seagal he could have 'em, but fuck it," said Irving. "I've got a feeling about this. Boychik, you kill on Carson, you just might be bigger than Cantinflas!"

Such acclaim from the man tithing a compulsory 10 percent of David's worth was, in the mind of David, taken from the same playbook of promises that He had once made about how the seed shall be prosperous, and the vine shall give her fruit, and the ground shall give her increase, and the heavens shall give their dew, and yada yada yada all that Peaceable Kingdom crap. But still, the idea of Irving caring enough to lie was as a salve to David's spirits, wounded now for forty-one nights and days.*

"Really?" confirmed David.

"Really," reconfirmed Irving, and he instructed his young client to go and ready himself to make mirth, which David did by finding Suzi again, for she had proved herself multi-mirthful.

---

* In fact, I suffered only three nights of disappointment before Johnny Carson called me out to be a guest. On the morning of that fourth day, I spoke to my mother, who said, "Maybe, honey, they're just going to say your name, and maybe they don't want you on the show."

31

⸙

In God's world, it was all good. And why not? When you're the Lord God Almighty, you can entertain yourself anytime you want, any way you want—for instance, by saying Benicio Del Toro three times real fast, or Googling "Madeleine Albright and Spring break"—for such are the rules of Almightiness and Self.

His peoples, however, now that was another issue. Most of them took themselves and their paltry lives too seriously, believing that what they did mattered in the Big Scheme of His things (see: Oscars and "brave actors"). Such was the dark side of ego that He had not foreseen when He created self-awareness at the same time as pubic hair, therefore giving neither of them the careful attention to detail they deserved; this, He now had to agree, might have been a (cough) mistake (cough). Alas, according to the spreadsheet He'd run, taking a mulligan on either of those, especially pubic hair, would create too many disruptions in the whole cosmic schmeer; and then having to make a bunch of little tweaks here and there as accommodations, well, He might as well do a page-one rewrite (see: Finger in the Dike)—and truly, those days were behind Him now.

Indeed, it was after the first flood that He decided to swear off do-overs. And if He were going to start them again now, He'd frankly lead with the Arabs and all the liquid fossils worth eighty bucks a barrel He'd given them as a guilty pity gift after the whole Ishmael thing. That, even He could admit, had been a big fat cluster fuck. Alas, it was too late to do anything meaningful about it except to speed up global warming and, with a cleverness rare even for Him, give Al Gore the impression that people cause it and people can stop it. As if.

Oh, and He might also consider a second take on the ancillary costs and ramifications of inbreeding, which were probably a tad too high, considering. Sure, He'd had the best of intentions—getting His peoples to learn, albeit the hard way (see: wild mushrooms), that they ought to get out there and mingle, not stay at home all the time cocooning with the family. But it hadn't worked out so well in, for example, Mississippi and Nova Scotia, having created a lot of banjo players with big foreheads.

Then there was steroids, and the Democratic Party (oy, what happened?), and Kevin Federline. Not to mention the oversight about God's own sex life—i.e., He hadn't gotten any since the Big Bang. Oh, well, maybe in the director's cut.

But of all the design flaws, the one that seemed to have the worst unintended consequences (yeah, He'd thought that *those* were a good idea, too) was everyone's having diverse senses of humor. What had seemed like a good idea on the order of different skin colors and heights and lines of credit was soon proved a miscalculation turned black hole that eventually opened the door for puns and Jerry Lewis. (Girls not getting the Three Stooges is governed by a different canon. See: emotional maturity.)

Over the millennia, He had watched often with celestial dismay as too many of His peoples missed jokes that might have bound them pleasantly to others; or, worse, laughed in all the wrong parts and came off as stupid jackasses whom anybody normal wouldn't want to be in the same zip code with. And this had led to far more unpleasantness in their realm than even Andy Dick—and, come to think of it, had in fact resulted directly in Dick "Your lack of faith is disturbing" Cheney.

At last had been His realization—for He is not beyond a good satori now and then—that He could rectify the dangerous humor disparity but not upset the fragile equilibrium of their otherwise inconsequential lives by planting seeds here and there that would in a few decades grow into mushroom clouds of shared hilarity, akin to the old days when the Beatles pulled a seventy-one share on Ed Sullivan.

These seeds would not, He decided, be on the order of, say, Tori Spelling getting a makeover on *Pimp My Ride* or Al Sharpton's running for president; that would be too on the nose for His creative genius. Instead, they would be more traditionally Shakespearean—on the order of, come to think of it, Rosa Parks's bus ride leading to Al Sharpton's presidential run.

By all measures, His plan for increasing humor among His peoples had been going surprisingly well; better, certainly, than Bruce Jenner's plastic surgeries. Truly, not since that little thing called the Inquisition, when the French put the Talmud on trial and burnt it at the stake, had He felt so much potential for amusement from the free will of they who had been made in His likeness yet somehow gave *Dances With Wolves* an Oscar.

Of course, He had to admit that, try as He might, there might never be another universally accepted instigator of belly yuks like a good old-fashioned rip-snorting fart, which throughout the ages had sent kings and commoners alike into conniptions of laughter. This was especially so among the English, for whom a good cheese cutting brings more joy than edible food and dentistry. Yea, even His yellow-skinned peoples (for whom tomfoolery does not exist in any other form) and His Teutonics (who find knee-buckling pleasure only in the misfortune of others) greet with boisterous enthusiasm the polyphonies of vigorous wind breaking. Indeed, at no age of their lives do any of His peoples achieve maturity enough to let the duck call of the anus pass unlaughed upon. Such has it been so since He created flatulence on that otherwise uneventful ninth day.

But hark and also hallelujah came now opportunity: In the old country formerly known as Mesopotamia, now under new management, had a leader called Saddam arisen to power under the old Mussolini rules of engagement and named his sons Uday and Qusay—Pig Latin!

Oh, God foresaw much future joviality with this Hussein family as well as their offspring-of-Ishmael brethren. And to ensure it He further surrounded them geographically with friends and enemies who had rejected the lead in *Texas Chainsaw Massacre* because their faith does not permit romantic comedies, onscreen or off. Great things were expected of them in the future, especially the tall bearded one with hundreds of siblings whose middle name "bin" is not capitalized—and to thoroughly ensure it, God retracted his first five inches of manhood. This He had long ago established as the anti–Uncle Miltie syndrome, in which a man with yardage to spare may feel free to dress like a woman, while a man with none to hold must feel compelled to slaughter a woman. (See also: "Small dicks and large trucks.")

Meanwhile, in the terrain of New Jersey, men with such jovial names as Johnny No Toes and Carmine the Sausage had turned their industrial attentions to the art of cinema and were at that moment casting a film starring a clitoris, one situated in the throat. This promised to rewrite the worldwide geography of humor as completely as Ozzy Osbourne would recontextualize sobriety. Indeed, what first drew God's attention to Jersey, and frankly impressed the Almighty in a way He had not been since realizing that Jews really do run the world, was the boys' knowing that "Genesis" had once been the word for "Yeah, just like that, but a little faster"; for He had originally placed Eve's pleasure center right there in the same spot before relocating it due south as Adam's punishment following the apple incident. How, you may wonder, did that punish Adam? Well, if Eve suddenly now couldn't swallow something that tasted sweet and pleasant while also moving the earth for her, she sure as hell wasn't going to swallow anything that didn't while not. Thus was birth given to dinner and a movie at least, as well as Brazilian waxing.

This mismatching of physiologies had once seemed like

a good idea to Him. But after enduring millennium after millennium of the same basic joke ("Question: How many Jewish girls does it take to give a blow job? Answer: Don't make me laugh"), He could see that His peoples' sense of humor, and therefore the world, might benefit from a new genital paradigm. And if the clitoris film turned out half as good as the auditions were going, this would be the catalyst for that paradigm (which was by the way a nonsense word He coined during the '70s after taking est). What He foresaw was resounding laughter from His multitudes across the great landscape as the film's potent message reached far and wide—in fact, all the way under the Oval Office desk, where a young woman who ought not to have worn a thong would search during stolen moments for the vast right-wing conspiracy and find that by bobbing on her knees she could bring a future president to his. (This was, of course, the posture that the current president, author of the distinctly unfunny long national nightmare, preferred his country to be in, though without the reciprocal pleasure.)

And oh, yes, there was also that lazy wannabe comedian David Steinberg, about whom God had mostly forgotten. Well, maybe not forgotten; more like lost interest in, He having been disappointed time and again with the lack of effort the kid had put out—less, even, than Alice Cooper, who at least cared enough about success to bite off the head of a bat. Only out of residual respect for Their one-time relationship—and His lingering hope that David would someday redeem himself by not just winging it with that bullshit improv when he got on stage—had God not put David on his Wrath To-Do List, turning him into a greeter at the Fort Lee Red Lobster, or Eva Braun's masseur.

But wasn't it so that David's nonchalance and insouci-
ance had been what attracted God to him in the first place?
And that now those were precisely what annoyed God
enough to go and create Ryan Seacrest? Yes, and He had
only Himself to blame for familiarity breeding contempt
(see: Sharon Stone's vagina in *Basic Instinct 2*). Which was
why He already had an Eye on another young man devoted
to the offbeat causing of laughter, one who wasn't at all
reluctant to put it out there for success but also had an easy
way, especially with himself—someone destined one day
for a full profile on the *E! True Hollywood Story*. Whom
would He choose to be His hootchie-cootchie boy, David
or this Pee-wee Herman fella? That was the question. And
the answer might require a coin flip. David had history
on his side, having been a key part of His original Plan.
But Pee-wee had so much going for him in so many ways.
Hmmm. Maybe there was a way to have both. Then He
could go back to figuring out why the evangelicals refused
to give Him credit for evolution. (Earth, six thousand years
old? Hah! He takes power naps longer than that.)

32

nd so came to pass at last, thank God, the tonight
on which David Steinberg appeared first on *The
Tonight Show,* in the one-man performance role
of a polysexual hillbilly who finds Scientology and lands
the coveted role of Elijah Wood's kosher vegan cook.* And

---

* What I performed on the show was a bit titled "How to Win a Best
Friend" in which my character conversed with a female voice, appearing to come from a phonograph record, that instructed me in how to
make a friend. The bit concludes with the voice saying, "I want to be
your best friend," and my lonely character, suffused with enthusiasm
and emotion, agreeing, "I want to be your friend, too." To which the
voice says, "I want to be your friend to the end . . . to the end . . . to the
end," as though the record had broken. This was the cue for me—still
in my unfunny Chaplinesque phase and not yet in my Grouchoesque
irreverent phase—to go for the pathos and toddle off like the Little
Tramp. The female voice, in fact, was not a recording. It belonged to
another performer live backstage—the luscious, leggy, delicious Carly

lo, David's humor slayed at least the host of TV hosts, who laughed with pleasure and surprise at the ten unusual minutes and led the applause of his audience, who in such way were encouraged to develop affection for David Steinberg. And when later came notice backstage that the host desired soon, nay, next week to have the comedian stand again on that stage in the performance of more original comedy, David explained that he would be unable now to accept the munificence but would be pleased to on his return from prior commitments: an international scouting trip to find babealicious racks for the *SI* swimsuit issue; as opening act for the Wu Tang Clan on a twelve-city tour of Jewish Homes for the Aged; and a private command performance for someone named Kevorkian, who desired to hear David's killer material.

And these were lies only in the fact that they were not true, for David desired above all not Johnny Carson to know that he possessed no further material for standing onstage alone in the service of causing laughter as do other professional comedians; and that he required time to write and perform and bomb and hone and perform and bomb a little less and write some more and perform until he bombed not at all over the course of ten minutes—and that would take, oh, three months.

And this was what in fact transpired, and then did

Simon, whose stage fright kept her from even coming out to take a bow. This was just months before her singing made her the biggest star on the planet. Which only proves once again that the ways of the Lord are unfathomably mysterious, for if this gorgeous woman had indeed appeared onstage with me, no one would ever have noticed David Steinberg. And that would have been that.

David return to that stage and again cause laughter from the mouth and quivering from Johnny Carson, who was as vigorously attentive as if observing Tara Reid on Ed McMahon's stripper pole. But David did not comprehend clearly the host's excellent response, for he believed that he was performing with less distinction even than the Rosenbergs on cross-examination.

Then did he bring to a close his six minutes with a description of Harvey Weinstein finding Heather Locklear on Jdate, and now did the audience imply their pleasure with cries of "huzzah," which to David's puzzled ears sounded exactly like "Get off the fucking stage, douchebag!" So when Mr. Carson motioned David to his side, David understood not the intention, nor what this may portend, for his addled mind could not see what all others could see: that the man was visibly delighted.

Slowly did David advance across the stage to sit tepidly alongside the host, feeling like Sergeant Preston of the Yukon at a celebrity Botox tournament—a notion that when conveyed aloud to the host extracted from him further hoots of laughter, as did his aloud wonderings why kreplach was not on the menu at Hooters and whether *enema* was a Jewish word. O, sweet theology. David discovered that he had but to open his mouth and let words tumble from it in order to evoke from Mr. Carson and his audience a welcome appreciation and approval, with laughs more in abundance than postwar Italian governments— though it remained the profoundest mystery to him, akin to the popularity of Pauly Shore movies, why the host and audience acted in response as they did to these witticisms, for they seemed to him as thin as Nicole Richie. But such was it so, and it would be fine not to have to take that gig as Dakota Fanning's on-set Hebrew teacher.

Now then did Mr. Carson delay the introduction of his next celebrity icons, Helen Keller and Andrea Bocelli, scheduled to sing an inspirational duet of "Amazing Grace." But in the green room they were to remain, insisted the host, who was desirous at this moment of further yuks from David.

This then became the moment on Mr. Carson's couch of David's celebrity consecration, as the host sanctified the comedian in the mind of America, and forever would nothing be the same, especially sexually. And thus did David know that he would not, any longer, have to be considered Winnipeg's answer to Wayne and Schuster.

"Great news, boychik," said Irving. "I can get you a six-episode guest arc on *Chico and the Man*."

33

Their names were Jack Benny and Milton Berle and George Burns, and there was another of them who had many brothers, and eyebrows the size of bongo drums, and a mustache the shape of Lassie, and a far better sex drive than the young King David, who would not lie with Abishag, though she was a fair damsel. And this man answered to the name Groucho, and you can bet Groucho would have lain with Abishag, or Gabishba, or Windbag, or Carmen Electra, or any other fair damsel, and even some not so fair, as well as others less fair even than Oscar Hammerstein—hell, he would've done any Female this side of Margaret Dumont, which in some ways made him Charlie Sheen but without the restraining order. And apparently this was from where derived Groucho's inclination toward inducing the laughter of others, for it was a sublimating sense of humor, kind of angry when you think about it, aimed at redirecting the fire in his loins, though it did not seem to be so to him, for you can also bet that when God wants something to stay sub rosa, it stays sub rosa.

But this is all much beside the point, which is that Benny and Berle and Burns and Marx and others who lacked foreskin and knew the meaning of the word *kibbitz*, which they enjoyed to do with each other, had been prevented by cruel prejudice from doing so along the sand traps of a golf course by those of blond hair and nice noses who feared the desecration of their Jew-free havens with the wrong element whose monthly bar tabs would be too little. And so had the Semites in response said "Fuck the goyim. We'll open our own club. What could be so hard? We'll get a little land and some Mexicans to mow the lawn."

And thus had they founded their own haven, open to all, with much better pin placement, on the Crest of a hill in the hills of Beverly, and there it was that they met daily to kibbitz, as was their wont, this Benny and Berle and Burns and Groucho—and now among them were they joined by David, whom they had acquired in the later rounds of the comedians' draft. Which in David's mind was the equivalent of Deepak Chopra getting Vishnu to give him a four-hand job.*

---

* For two years I met Groucho Marx, George Burns, and Jack Benny every Tuesday for lunch at Hillcrest Country Club. In all those times I could never erase from my mind two vital questions: *How the fuck did I get here to be with these guys?* And, *Who must they think I am?* It was never not a surreal experience. Neither did I understand why these colossally successful entertainers in their seventies and eighties sometimes raged for hours about some minor critic at, say, the *Philadelphia*

And in the company of these men did David revel in dialogues of humor for which he gave as good as he got, and this was good—very good. Oy, was it good. And at first when they spoke he would chuckle helplessly with appreciation at their uttered lines of superior amusement for which the only viable response was shoulder-shaking yucks, for these remarks were the highest expressions of hilarity in all the land. But each time came the audible mirth from his mouth, one of the living legends would look quickly to the others, annoyed, just as Robert De Niro turned in mock disgust to Tessio when don Roberto the landlord offered to keep the rent the same; for in this world in which comic words were lethal weapons and also a nice living for some of them, laughter was strictly a civilian thing; only audiences were allowed, of course encouraged, to react in this way. On professionals, such behavior was frowned. Unless they were telling dick jokes at a Friar's Club roast of Uncle Miltie, professionals learned to keep their laugh inside, unuttered, where at first it might hurt

Inquirer, who'd panned them fifty years ago at a time when they were the toast of the country and giants like Shaw and Ionesco were kissing the hem of their jackets. I couldn't get over that everyone had loved them except for this one little pisher—and five decades later the little pisher was all they remembered. Well, in 1968, I received a review in the *Washington Post* of my engagement at the Cellar Door that began: "David Steinberg is funny, but . . . " The little pisher who wrote that was present at another Steinberg Cellar Door show debut on the same evening that one Chip Taylor was opening, too. He wrote: "There were two openings tonight, one by a performer of talent and wit, the other by a witless hack. Chip Taylor is a performer who will be heard from for years to come. David Steinberg is not worth writing about."

their *kishkes* as it struggled to emerge and express itself.* And if they absolutely had to, they were permitted to state, in a plain, calm voice, as though commenting on the fine weather today, "That's funny." For there could be nothing so humorous articulated by another member of this inner circle as to elicit the laughter that they lived to hear from paying spectators.†

And when at last David had mastered this form of self-repression, and had himself heard from each of them

---

* I was once asked to emcee a Friar's Club roast of Milton Berle, who raised a big stink to the club's board that I wouldn't be dirty enough. His fears, though, were allayed the night of the roast when I introduced the first roaster, Slappy White, as "the last person to get a blow job from Moms Mabley." The festivities quickly became a symphony of dick jokes, as comedian after comedian exhausted the subject of Berle's legendary member with every variation imaginable. The final roaster, appropriately, was Dick Shawn. I felt almost apologetic as I walked him to the dais, knowing that there could be nothing left to say. But Shawn had an advantage over the other comedians. The man's comedy was visual; he painted pictures with words. Taking a long deep breath, he began, "*I* actually got to see it. It was at the Friar's Club in New York. Milton was in the steam bath. I thought he was there with his son."

† Though Groucho had told me that he preferred "a darkie behind the wheel," I often picked him up, driving him to and from our Tuesday lunches at Hillcrest. On our way out of the dining room one day, Groucho asked if I wanted to meet Adolph Zukor, the legendary founder of Paramount Pictures. I said sure, and Groucho led me toward where Zukor was sitting. At that point he was almost hundred (he died in 1976 at 103) and looked like a cap in a chair. Groucho bent down, pointed at me, and shouted, "Adolph! You remember Chico, don't you?"

"That's funny, kid" at least once and with truth and admiration, the legend they called Groucho asked of David to compose in script, for performance on the Broadway stage, the legend of the legend and the legend's legendary family, Gummo included. And this was a surprise to David, who had not committed words to paper since dropping acid and writing that poem ("You can be anyone anywhere in everywhere there / you can be anyone anything anytime anywhere / everywhere is here in everywhere there") for which he'd won a Rod McKuen fellowship at ITT Tech* and a $50 Starbucks gift card. But he accepted the honor from the living legend with honor and now, for research's sake, legitimately had excuse to attach himself to Mr. Groucho as Jesse Jackson clings to the past.

And it was at the home of the legend on the hill high above the hills of Beverly where David dined with and talked to and heard from other legends who had shared with this legend a legendary time past yet whose wisdom and sophistication graced still the pages of the nation's reading material and the screens of their viewing; and yea, this close association with them as well was better in the mind of David, who was no starfucker, than hitting a frat kegger with Michael Eisner. For these were men whose

---

* Rod McKuen followed me as a guest one night on *The Tonight Show*. At the end of my final segment, Johnny Carson offhandedly asked me, "What do you think of Rod McKuen?" I replied, "He's my second-favorite poet." Knowing instinctively that he shouldn't take this further, Carson did a look into the audience that got a huge laugh. Then he added, "Okay, I'll bite. Who's first?" Having by then moved out of my Chaplin phase and into my Groucho years, I said: "Everyone else." McKuen never forgave me. Can't say I blame him.

likenesses appeared on the Mount Rushmore of conversation and were yet at the apogee of fame.

Understand that it was not their conversation that most necessarily enchanted them to David but the fact that sometimes they would be accompanied by their daughters who were (for explanations that David concluded had to do with mothers who themselves, attracted to such men of prestige and wit, had been such 10s before they were replaced by increasingly younger and firmer versions attracted to such men of prestige and cash) blessed in the genes department. And rarely, except for occasionally if they were married, did David fail to score with these daughters. Most memorably, there was that time when two of them, not twins, but each a dead ringer for Jacqueline Bisset wearing a wet t-shirt with nipples erect in *The Deep*, sat adjacent to each other, across the table from David. And as he listened intently and with reverence to the speaking of their father (a man who cannot be named here in the blasphemous text for he is an intellectual yet amongst the living who believes devoutly in defamation litigation and 9mm pistols as instruments of social change and sport) did David extend his legs under the table toward each of them, kicking off his loafers as he did so, to play biblical footsie, for he desired to know them pedally. And by coffee and strudel he had slid his stockinged feet up, up, up and placed a big toe into each of their vaginas, finding in them happy homes and grateful owners. And they both loved him, and later he loved them both, though sequentially, alas, for they would not love each other.

Aside from such irritations, David had become Spartacus, leaving each victory with a larger retinue of admirers—all for reasons far beyond his comprehension. There were dinner parties with Neil Simon and Swifty Lazar and Sidney Lumet and Orson Welles at which he was seated next to Jackie O; television appearances on the host of hosts' show whenever he or the host was so inclined; SRO nightclub engagements in Jonesboro, Arkansas; groupies who orgasmed at hello; a foursome with the Gabor sisters; skinny-dipping with the cast of *The Barbi Benton Show*; gold-key passes to the Playboy mansions in Chicago and L.A. along with a reserved alcove in the grotto; his very own bold-face name plaque from Page Six; a directory of all other celebrities' unlisted phone numbers, including first-dial privileges for Keira Knightley's twenty-first birthday; invitations from Joe Papp to do Richard III in the park as a bipolar Christian Scientist ("Some lithium! Some lithium! My kingdom for some lithium"); courtside seats to the Knicks and a soapbox for political opinions; private tutoring in the secret celebrity handshake; Wayne and Schuster's old table at Elaine's; tabloid reporters picking through his garbage; preliminary interest from Calvin Klein; all the swag he could carry out of awards shows; places of honor in the St. Paddy's Day and Columbus Day parades, and Park Slope Purim Pageant; free lifetime membership in the Elders of Zion and a signed-framed Xerox of the world-domination plan; sudden disdain for flyover country; a mere three degrees of separation from anyone of note in the entire world; a standing appointment with and the home number of Dr. Feelgood; a top-ten listing on Nixon's enemies list; free passes on a fashion faux

34

∽⸙∽

o, pleasure was ordinary life now for young David, for whom all opportunities seemed realities. The days of selling his plasma for bus fare—well, he had never suffered days like that, though during one long night of despair he had been forced to drink the raspberry-flavored Vitaminwater when the concierge idiotically failed to stock his minibar with passion fruit; and he had once forgotten to don his special protective glasses before staring directly at Keith Richards's face, which, *kanehora*, could have turned out a whole lot worse than it did (see: Medusa). There was also that mysterious time *US Weekly* mistook him for Regis Philbin. And then came the effect of a double-dose roofie Martha Stewart had slipped him at her free-at-last party. Oh, and for several months he'd had to deny playing for the other team when he casually wondered why the "d" in DiCaprio was inappropriately capitalized.

pas from Anna Wintour; and his name dropped by people he'd never met. PBS even asked him to host pledge breaks during a Dr. Wayne Dwyer special. Yes, life was good for David Steinberg.

"But something is missing," he mused aloud to himself one early dawn when it had been five long hours since the opiate of applause and six long minutes since the third expert servicing that night of the Prohobska twins.

And when the Almighty overheard these words of David's (which He is permitted by the Cosmic Act of 14^8 B.C.), God puffed out His chest, pleased that David missed Their relationship and—oops, in the moment that followed He learned something about pride leading to falls, something that now made Him want to give a shout-out of regret and empathy to Icarus (and also the Baldwin brothers). For God's pride was premature: David was not aloud lamenting too little God and meaning in his life, nor too much mindless sex, for he had discovered that that was some of the best kind—and besides, what was too much? No, the young comedian meant neither of those things.

"Basketball," declareth David, completing his musing. "I miss basketball."

Basketball? God was as stunned to hear this from David as He had been to witness that Father Anyone missed masturbation during his term at St. Anus Seminary.

Yet the Almighty was not in a punishing mood, which seemed a surprise given the evidence that He does not endure disappointment particularly well (see: Golden Calf and Forty Years in the Desert). Sure, His first inclinations were to shrink David's penis to the size of a quark or rip him a new one in the forehead, but then He reflected on the fact that He, after all, had been the One to make David as he is—a typical Leo. And had not He also chosen David for this comedy gig precisely because he is as he is, just as He is the way He is (a Gemini—duh!)? And had not David been previously occupied on the court of b-ball, practicing his crossover dribble, when first He had approached him? Yes, yes, yes. Which meant to God that David deserved to continue his basketball career, though modified, on a parallel track with Hollywood, which had come to employ David now and then, when he was between tours or had tired temporarily of comparing the president of the United States to Joey Buttafuoco (but without the charm).

Thus did David receive a message one July morning in the most central park of New York, where he was earning a modest amount of lucre to canoodle on camera with an actress soon to be renowned by her name Susan Sarandon, and this was a role for which David had no discernible talent other than his desire to spend the hot summer close to the breasts of Susan Sarandon and pretend an affection for her and them which he did not have to pretend, which made of him a far better actor, for he possessed not the thespian skill to fool the camera were it not so.*

---

* I would like to say that 1979's *Something Short of Paradise*, in which I co-starred with Susan Sarandon, is considered a classic. Alas, when it's considered at all, it isn't considered much of anything other than the film the gorgeous and sexy Ms. Sarandon was in before rubbing lemons on herself in *Atlantic City*. Each time I watch *Paradise*, which I do occasionally for medicinal purposes, I can see myself straining in every scene. No, not straining to remember my method. Straining not to be aroused. There is no Stanislavski for that.

"Call Dave DeBusschere," said the message on pink paper which came hand-delivered to him courtesy of an oversized and undermodest PA whose chest bore the tattooed lyrics of "To All the Girls I've Loved Before." Upon reading the message inscribed with the name of a hoops player of Hall of Fame achievement, David assumed he could trust its truth as June Cleaver trusted Eddie Haskell, for David knew not Dave DeBusschere as a man; but he did know that the young assistant believed it should be he shtupping Susan Sarandon on camera and that all he had to do to make the producers and director see the light shine upon the error of their miscasting ways was to remove David temporarily from the premises.

Yo, these were the days when the equipment existed not to return telephone calls from a hip pocket, and in the centralized park of New York the placing of a return call from a stationary upright cabinet costing a dime required pedestrian transit several thousand Mesopotamian cubits away. Were he to endure this trek between moments when his presence was required, David would therefore be absent the location premises long enough for the coup, which he feared not but which caused him reasonably to suspect that this fucking PA was trying to pull some other kind of shit. So he went not to return the call.

But soon came a second message from the same Dave DeBusschere at the same alleged return phone number, and this message was delivered by a second PA with whom David had smoked some Thai stick and discussed at length and in depth the archetypal significance of bobblehead dolls on a post–Katie Couric *Today* show, and whether Frankie Muniz could fit completely between Teri

Hatcher's breasts. So David trusted the man. And took the number. And between takes donned his sandals for the walk. And dialed. And spoke to Dave DeBusschere, who proclaimed that he had heard of David's legendary prowess with the round ball—which was not just puny celebrity prowess but 152nd Street and Broadway prowess—and he invited David to partake in a three-on-three tournament in Vegas.

Know well that David felt flattered to be so thought of as the Jew legend of Winnipeg-Harlem playgrounds, and the idea of playing on a team with a retired professional and current professional this weekend was, it can be said, far more exciting than when God first knocked on the door of his mind as he practiced his blind wraparound. But alas, he would have to say no, David said, for his producers were three young dickheads who reminded him daily that he had been an abomination of miscasting; they believed it was not believable that Ms. Susan Sarandon would enjoy herself with him sexually, which was called for in the script, and that if it were not for Ms. Sarandon herself offering them assurances that she most certainly would, David would've been toast and could spend the rest of his life opening for Myron Cohen at the Pewter Saddle lounge for all they fuckin' cared.

"It's kind of tenuous around here," said David to Mr. DeBusschere, who spoke truth to power in his reply.

"Winners get ten grand," replied Mr. DeBusschere. "Each."

"Each?"

"Each."

Which was thrice the amount for which David had

been salaried for his present employment by the three dickheads. So now when came Friday afternoon's wrap did a cab arrive with Mr. DeBusschere and another legend of greatness known as "The Pearl," whom Mr. DeBusschere introduced as Earl Monroe, which shocked the holy shit out of the producers' watchful eyes. And off drove they to the place from which air transport originates, and this being in the epoch before the white zone was for the loading and loading of aggravation only, they arrived in time for their appointment with destiny in the hanging chad of American cities.

For David, this was the promised land, to see players whom he had admired once and admired now today in an assemblage, and there were many whose names would last forever in public admiration and fame, and these were some of their names: Dr. J, Maurice Lucas, David Thompson, Walt Frazier, Kevin Loughery, Calvin Murphy, and there were also famous men of Hollywood accomplishment who had game—and also height on David. But as the game played was three-on-three, located on half the court, not five-on-five, located on the full court, the strategies of shoot and pick were well known to and well practiced by David, on whose team was Mr. Paul Westphal and Mr. Sam Jones; and over these two days they smited all the others to win the booty.

"Steinberg has ice water in his veins," declared Mr. DeBusschere from behind the microphone in his call of the final game, as David slashed through the key and put up the contest-winning hook, which was the least impressive move he'd made in two days.

Hallelujah, David had already accomplished much,

and there would be yet more to accomplish, but this would be his greatest story ever told. And unlike the other greatest stories ever told, it had the advantage of being true. And he would always have the video to enjoy. (See: Gloria Swanson.)*

---

* My friends claim that I watch the tape of my tournament-winning performance alongside Sam Jones and Paul Westphal with the same glory-days nostalgia of Norma Desmond ogling herself on the silent screen. This is not quite true. The videotape is in color.

35

And in time David said farewell to fantastic mind-less sex with an inventory of women envied even by God, for he had had much of it, and though not *too* much, he believed not that his memories of those numerous moments would sustain forever but that he would be no longer in need of such extraordinary suste-nance, having now beheld and held the woman whose love he believed would maintain him forever instead. And she was not a girl who counted Sarah and Rebecca and Rachel as foremothers, for her forebears named Angela, Lucretia, and Magdalena hailed from the land of pasta; and for a long time pizza on matzo was enjoyed in the Steinberg home *abbondanza* and all was good. And then arrived two beautiful daughters, and all was well and happy, save those too many times when David was onstage and too far from them all. Often came the moment when those with whom he had been acquainted in the long past would arrive backstage with flowers and kisses and compliments and their children following a show in which he seemed to have induced hilarity in the assembled; and many would tell him of their observation that he had climbed the mountain of success and planted his own flag at its summit. But David felt not worthy of their florid words, for in envy he would see them with their children and their beloveds, and he would hunger that he were now with those he loved instead of with those who loved him onstage while knowing him not, not really. And apparently God heard, for in time the flag lowered from the mountain.

To everything there was a season, and a time for every purpose; and some seasons and some purposes were more agreeable than others but lasted not as long as those that were not. For when came the season of misery between David and his wife, that season was followed by another season of misery, then another; and soon they saw that there would be no other season except misery as long as they remained in marriage with each other. But leave her, he would not, for he rathered by far that his children be happy than he not be miserable.

And the years passed, though not the seasons, until came the day when David's wife chose to end the misery between them in exchange for what was behind Door Number Three. Thus it was written, thus it was done. And frequent were the surprises behind that door.

36

It came to pass that there occurred many trades between Canada and America, and America enjoyed the better end of them, sending away draft dodgers and the uninsured and receiving those of talent and wit with eager ambitions to share their wit and talent to a wider world, which was why they got the hell out of there as soon as they could. And their leavings by the thousands left a dearth in the northern land where once a dearth had been anyway, for there are not so many people there. And David Steinberg noticed that dearth, and so he returned to his ancestral homeland to help shovel into it much-needed entertainments which had been lost by the talent exodus. And he achieved that by introducing the new medium of television, which Canadians had heard of but not seen unless you count guys in Elmer Fudd hats getting shitfaced on Molson and telling stupid-American jokes. (See: Wayne and Schuster.) Thus did David bring laughter and joy to Canadians across the wide swath of Great North—except for the Quebecois, who preferred to watch Guy Lafleur and Pierre Trudeau interview each other on Channel Deux in reruns of *The Only Two Famous French Canadians, Eh, Show.*

O, Lord of the Chia Pet and other amusements, David's program of various varieties of comedy was renowned across the tundra for its clever premises in a series of episodes that joined the funny-bone antics of NASCAR with the freshness of *Gigli,* and the show had the emotional effect on its viewers of Mohammed cartoons on Danish welfare recipients.

And yea, David was joined in stage presence by many people of humor talent whom he dragged along with him from south of the tundra. And these were some of their names: Tom Smothers, Avery Schreiber, Scatman Crothers, Milton Berle, Ethel Merman, Jon Voight, James Coco, Rip Taylor, Robert Vaughn, Michele Lee, Peggy Cass. And too, many others of various talents who had been born and resided still in the tundra joined him with frequency on the show (as opposed to those who resided legally south and beat it out of there as soon as their shows wrapped), and these were some of the northerners' names: Martin Short, Catherine O'Hara, Joe Flaherty, John Candy, Andrea Martin. And they of the North Country were well loved and very well laughed at (though not so well compensated) for their comedic talents which brought so much enjoyment to their fellow Great North citizens who had tuned into *The David Steinberg Show;* and that level of adoration and talent of course eligibled them for green cards so that they could make exodus to the south, which of course they did at the earliest possible opportunity. So, of course, the dearth returned to the north. (Maybe that is to be expected when the administrator of the so-called free national health care system is Mary Baker Eddy.)*

---

* *The David Steinberg Show*, not to be confused with *The David Steinberg Show* (a summer replacement variety show on CBS), was produced and aired in Canada on CTV, the Canadian national network. Though it was both well reviewed and widely viewed, the satire on talk shows is remembered primarily as the launching pad for the actors who would soon form SCTV, because it was canceled after only one season in order to make room for *Stars on Ice*. So when someone asks me why every Canadian comedian eventually heads to the States, the answer is *Stars on Ice*.

37

allelujah, when the wind was correct, and God actually remembered to tend His plan, there was a divine miracle of broadcast signal bleed to the far south that brought the message of David Steinberg's television entertainments to the highly refined audience residing upstate at Green Haven correctional facility. This captive audience of savants had made of David an entertainer worth fighting over—though without the usual shivs hidden in their socks. Such fact was revealed to David through another of the Almighty's practical jokes that may or may not have been part of the Plan™, which He has little reason or desire to reveal, unlike filmmakers who are strangely proud to take the SFX mystery out of movies with behind-the-scenes looks.

In one of those movies there had been an actor known to the world as Jerry Orbach, who had enjoyed the portraying of a man who took no offense to being known as one of the "boys" so long as the ones doing the knowing were *his* boys and not *those* boys from other turf, like the Colombo boys, or the Genovese boys, whom he preferred to smite with extreme prejudice, and vice versa; nor did such particular boys as he take offense at nicknames like the Chin, the Horse, the Wop, the Turk, the Icepick, for these were given with affection, not garrotes. And this man who was also one of the boys was called affectionately Crazy but with the advantage, unlike the others, of having it precede his other names; thus he was Crazy Joe Gallo, his nickname as earned as the Icepick's.

But Mr. Orbach in his portrayal of Crazy had searched for the sanity and love and the tenderness beneath the murdering craziness, for that is what actors do, which explains why they tend to believe always that Cain and Don Corleone and Jack Henry Abbott are also lovely in their hearts. So when came the day that Crazy Joey walked out of the prison he stepped into the recuperative arms of Mr. Orbach and Mrs. Orbach, who were beloved by all who knew them, men and women of accomplishment whose tongues sang with wit and maybe a little gossip, too. And on Sabbath afternoons their abode was as open to friends for a little nosh as David Gest's motives are open to interpretation.

Then on one Sunday did David, for whom Jerry Orbach felt inexplicable affection, enter the Orbach salon and become greeted by the host with these words: "David, Joey Gallo's out and Marta and I think he's totally rehabbed." And this was the word David Steinberg spoke in reply:

"Bullshit."

"Sssh," mandated Jerry, for Joey Gallo was nearby and his bodyguard was nearer even. "He'll hear you."

"Joey Gallo's here?"

"Yeah, and there's only one person he's really interested in meeting."

"Good," saith David, "because I'm not interested in meeting him."

"Well," replied Jerry, "you're the one he wants to meet."

And this was seven-years-of-famine news from David's point of view, and he sought to depart before his Timex struck the next second. But Jerry Orbach said, "Depart not, David," for at that moment stood Crazy Joey's bodyguard in front of David, and the smile on his face without mirth looked like the last thing many see in this life. And the man held his countenance steadfastly until did David turn in the pointed direction to behold Crazy Joey, a man whose eyes could read a room as only those whose final moments might be always a single muzzle flash away could read a room.

Now then rose Crazy Joey to greet David. "Oh," said he, "I've been looking forward to this."

"How do you know me?" asked David of Crazy Joey.

"Are you kidding?" responded Crazy onto David. "We used to fight to get to watch you on the tube in the joint."

"Me?"

"Yeah, everybody loved you. Especially the [men blessed with a second helping of melanin in their skin]. The only ones who didn't like you were the Nazis."

"That's a relief."

"Fuck 'em anyway. They wouldn't know how to laugh if you paid 'em off."

"I know, I've tried," said David.

Crazy responded with a sudden emanation indicating

gratification at the utterance of David, which David took to mean that after ten years in the slammer, Dennis Rodman, Dorothy Kilgallen, Kurt Cobain, Jerry Colonna, and Officer Krupke could have reduced Crazy Joey to helpless laughter by reciting the Dead Sea Scrolls.

"You know," said Crazy, "you'd do really well there."

"In prison?"

"Yeah, baby, you'd be a star."

"Well, it's good to always have something to fall back on," said David, causing now Crazy to steady himself from the chariot of helpless mirth that rolled over him as Lizzie Grubman mows down the unhot.

And so then did David wonder aloud to Crazy Joey whether those adversaries of Crazy's who had treated him as time had treated Mickey Rourke were yet in living existence—and, hearing that they were indeed yet breathing, he then wondered aloud whether they were yet attracted to the design of transforming Crazy into Brooklyn roadkill. Indeed they were, acknowledged Joey. And this of course indicated to David's quick and calculating mind that safety could be found only by observing a no-fly zone of three zip codes' radius around Crazy Joey. But though this was devoutly to be wished, it would not be so, for when Crazy Joey chose you as his BFF, you were indeed his best friend forever, bitch.

And this was not so terrible as it might seem, for while Crazy did not distinguish Pearl Jam from toe jam, and believed that velvet paintings of Elvis derive directly from the hand of Michelangelo, he proved himself a genial companion on occasions over the months—months in which David accompanied Mr. and Mrs. Orbach and Crazy Joey to establishments of nighttime amusements at locales where ethnic men of song received lucre for attracting diners willing to part with two drinks minimum that contain less spirits than Betty Ford's morning coffee and cost each more than a 1940s bar mitzvah.

And lo, one evening after witnessing the musical stylings of Mr. Buddy Greco, the Crazy entourage that included David awaited the boarding of the building's vertical train that would bound them to the performer's dressing room, where all would be received by the singer and offer him unlimited praise for his general virtuosity and blah blah blah. But when came the car into which they piled en masse, there appeared space not for David, who did not wish to suffer as sardines do and so ipso facto took backward a giant step with assurances that he would cometh when arrived the following car.

But this was not to be, for as the doors began their closing did Crazy Joey launch his arm into the path of the doors with the speed of Thelma and Louise's choice of shortcuts and attach onto David's arm with the insistence of foreign objects during Giuliani Time.

With suddenness did David find himself inside the vertical transport vehicle, ascending, his nose only demi-cubits from Crazy, whose eyes, David could now see, must have inspired incontinence in many.

Thus spake Crazy Joey with a touch of Simon Cowell in his tenor, "David, we're in Colombo territory here, and his guys know you're with me, so you can't be alone. If you get what I mean."

"This is Colombo territory?" asked David, for he was relieved that this was not Rupert Murdoch territory.

"The nightclubs—all of them. Whaddya think?"

"What do I think? I think you oughta tell me next time we're supposed to be in Colombo territory, so I can stay home."

Such utterance provoked giggles of approval from Crazy Joey, for he enjoyed David as the rich enjoy the Hamptons. And yea, David enjoyed Crazy Joey, too, but as Marilyn Manson enjoys an audience of evangelicals.

That which David preferred more was his own audience, and there appeared to be many in that audience who preferred his performance to the musical stylings of, let this be an example, Buddy Greco. Indeed, what had come to pass in the generations was a severe cleaving of entertainments, and this was not your father's zeitgeist. In his performances David preferred his audience to share with him the pleasure of a comedic bowel movement on the metaphoric person of the president of the United States, who was called Richard M. Nixon; and this quirk did not qualify David for appearances on stages where audiences belonging to a silent majority preferred musical mashed potatoes. And though the Boys whose mashed-potato-adoring stages these were would theoretically defend to the death David Steinberg's right to move a metaphoric bowel on the president, on their stages they would have preferred to slit the little Jew like a mackerel. And in this proclivity they were not alone.

For as it happened did card-carrying representatives of a lesser governmental agency known as the FBI emerge at the entrance to David's quarters sited on an upper floor of well-adorned lodgings known as the Plaza. Soon was David to perform downstairs in his yet most important

engagement at which there was no room at this inn for
they who had not been previously ticketed. Hallelujah, all
the glittering people and others were preparing to gather
this evening at extortionate cost for laughter and to see and
be seen by and by. But though David Fucking Steinberg's
name adorned the marquee, it was at this moment merely
David Steinberg in his stockings and underwear pigging
out under the influence of the munchies on the floor of
his haven when the G-men knocked and called out to him
their identities. Quickly then did David flush away that
which he was not prepared to be punished for possession
of. And now then did he open the door. And then did the
feds utter with ponderous significance and magnitude that
David's performance must not be performed tonight, for it
had come to their written attention that an undetermined
number of the ill-intended (they who were not amused by
David's verbal amusements) plotted to make of David a
burnt offering upon the performing dais.

Said the note which they did show to David, "And I
will bring distress upon him, that he shall walk like blind
men, because he has sinned against the president; and his
blood shall be poured out as dust, and his flesh as the dung.
Neither his silver nor his gold shall be able to deliver him
in the day of the Lord's wrath; but the whole stage shall
be devoured by the fire of his impertinence; for he shall be
made of a speedy riddance. Same with Boy George. And
also Elton John, that fag Jew. Who's he kidding? They
should be more like Barry Manilow."

And though in all his previous years the sum of David's
courage manifestations had numbered one, when that once
he refused the nitrous during a semiannual prophylaxis, yet

was he now suddenly imbued with the spirit of David Hasselhoff diving into a wave tank. No, he did not believe that God would surround him with an invisible Kevlar-type material capable of stopping a large-caliber bullet fired from a high-powered rifle out the window of a schoolbook depository (for this was back in the day when public schools actually provided books to their students and had to have a depository for them, so such a thought might naturally occur). Nor did David expect the Almighty to pluck the poisoned projectiles out of air, as only He could—and would have if, say, Moses were up there telling Canaanite jokes; alas, God had gone missing and was last seen enjoying a good Macchiato while watching the Hindu version of *One Life to Live* called *Too Many Lives to Suffer*. ("Oh, Gupta, you will surely never be able to get off the great wheel of birth and death with such karmic misbehaviors as these.")

Hallelujah, what David believed truly was that if his show was canceled, all that lucre in ticket sales would have to be refunded, and then where would it stop? One cancellation would follow another, for the assassin threateners would be emboldened to repeat their mischiefs, and soon his only gigs would be as dresser for *La Cage Aux Folles,* or audience warm-up for *The View.* Then opening for M. C. Hammer. And after that, blogging for Arianna Huffington. Which meant that flocks would lie down in the midst of the field, and all the beasts of the nations would devour them, and both the cormorant and the bittern would lodge in the upper lintels of whatever lintels have uppers of, and their voices would sing in the broken windows, crying of desolation in the thresholds or whatever. And this was a fate worse than a contractual obligation to appear in *Meet the Fockers* with no first-dollar gross points. By Zeus, there was only one choice of feat available to him.

And so on with the show did David proceed, appearing on the Plaza dais with jokes as planned and paid for, but also did he perform his humor while elevated atop a stool, which he explained to his audience made of him an easier target for Axis of Evil members who had seen *The Parallax View* and desired to go postal.

And there was about that night, with immediate violent passage to the other side of life possible or imminent, a heightened focus in the moment which made of David's concentration more keen; and closer for those moments did he feel to his maker; and then did he share with the audience an aside observation that merely an *s* separates *exist* from *exit*. And even though they believed that the whole fucking thing was a ruse he'd cooked up on acid— that weird they're-gonna-kill-me-so-I'll-get-up-on-a-chair martyr thing, like he had JFK-RFK-MLK envy or something—they each offered him the sound of two hands clapping hard for his effort before they beat a hasty exit so that the line at Scores would not be overly long, for surely, knowing David Steinberg, this was the *S* to which he had alluded.

O, there was joy and rejoicing and relief that followed the performance, for David had survived and aced; and now came to him the G-men to offer escort and safety to his upper-floor echelon; and overhearing of this was Crazy Joey, who spoke the truth to say, "David, believe me, I can protect you better than these doofuses."

And though the offer was tempting—because might not

those wishing to escort David safely be not the very messengers of violence and intolerance they claim protection from,
with nothing being what it seems—David insisted to Crazy
Joey that he would return with the doofuses instead. One
of them, he explained, did a dead-on Christopher Walken
impression that always cracked him up.*

---

* I know it sounds like an episode from *Goodfellas,* but episodes in
Goodfellas sound the way they do because things like this really hap-
pen—and all this happened exactly the way it's told, except for the
Christopher Walken impression. Actually, the guy did Cagney.

38

Then came to grow the desire of Crazy Joey Gallo for matrimony to Costanza the Womb, and the nuptials were prepared at the home of the husband and wife of whom all marriage aspirants within their concentric circles of acquaintance aspired to similar bliss, and they were the Orbach couple. Mr. Jerry Orbach requested fervently on behalf of the groom David's presence at the anointed hour, which had come on suddenly and without prior preprinted or embossed warning, as though the wand in the home-testing kit had just turned blue. But alas, replied David, he would be wholly engaged at that hour before television cameras with Mr. Johnny Carson and could not defer such appearance even to shoot Super Soakers with Halle Berry; he did, though, offer assurances of arrival with pleasure for festivities sometime, he presumed, following the moment when Crazy Joey had broken the glass or shot off an Uzi, or whatever was the observed custom for men of his persuasion.

Later then came the hour after David's performance on the imperative television program, and the moment when the lights they darkened in this studio did he feel more limp than had Jacob after attempting to sire all twelve tribes in one night. For truly had David Steinberg, Comedian, given his altogether out on the stage—and O, this was the utterly truthful sensation he expressed in a communication over the voice wires to Mr. Orbach by way of apologia for his yearning now to slumber rather than to make merry with goombahs. Surely, said David, the absence of a mere one among many revelers in the carousing hours after the nuptials, when surely the attendees were several sheets of Chianti too far to the wind for David ever to catch up anyway, would pass unnoticed by the groom; and surely would Crazy Joey be of forgiveness and order not a kneecapping of David for blowing off the party.

And surely, replied Mr. Orbach, did David jest: "They haven't even had the wedding yet," exclaimed he. "Joey's been waiting for you. David, you're the best man."

Oy, said David.

Thus did he endure a cab adventure purveyed by a graduate of the Kennedy & Sons School of Driving and Flying in order to arrive quickly at the Orbach home, where he greeted the groom with, "You had me at 'I do.'"

But in advance of performing his duties of best man, and with the caution of a pawnbroker offered a Rolex by some guy who pronounces it "Lorex," David sought the sage counsel of one Louie the Lip, who assured David that standing up for a made man did not of him also automatically make a target for dead trout on the windshield placed strategically as an inducement to fear by the aggrieved heirs of Colombo—he who now lay as dead as Whitney Houston's career from a bullet ordered by Crazy Joey. Or so believed the aggrieved and grieving.

And David agreed to accomplish that which was required of him, and Crazy Joey promised in return favors galore, which David wanted not, but all right, if insisted upon, he'd accept the tickets to see Helen Reddy and George Balanchine at the Shannon Doherty Auditorium, for he could always scalp them for twice face value to out-of-towners. Now, therefore, did Father Damian, the freelance man of God hired away from the leprosy convention, pronounce them Mr. and Mrs. Crazy, and Crazy Joey not only broke the glass, he chewed it and swallowed. And then there was much cheerful enjoyment into the early hours, when at last Louis Prima donned on his head a lampshade and sang "Hatikvah," which gave the pre–Vatican II diehards in the crowd a special shiver.

Soon then came Crazy Joey's birthday night in Colombo territory at the Copa in appreciation of Rickles the Insult Comic. And all present wished afterward to extend the enjoyment further and take it elsewhere, to a clam restaurant in the Village. Well, all present but David, of course, who noted that he needed to awaken tomorrow at the unholy hour of noon for a critically important game of hoops at the Y, and was anyway eager to get home and watch the *Gilmore, Spice, Indigo, and Golden Girls Gone Wild* on pay-per-view.

This refusal, argued the Orbachs, was not the act of a friend celebrating another friend's birthday. Had not Crazy Joey thought well enough of David to honor him with his best manhood? Such a refusal to drink the Kool-Aid at further festivities on a birthday, they insisted, was considered a mortal sign of disrespect in the great culture of Lucky Luciano and Notorious B.I.G.

"Hey, Crazy," called David. "You cool with me going home while you guys go on by yourselves?"

"Sure, David, whatever," spake Crazy.

But this acquiescence was insufficient attestation for the Orbach couple, who were devotedly committed to the rehabilitation of Crazy Joey through admiration and approbation. They halted David's in-progress egress with a quantity of pleading of the kind that David had not heard since he tried to convince Sharon Goldstein that it would be a cosmic error from which she would never recover to enter the seventh grade a virgin.

"David," said the Orbachs. "You saw *The Godfather*, right?"

"Yeah, so?" said David.

"Come on, wiseguys are major box office."

"Meaning what?"

"David, it's so obvious: Mafia is the new black."

There was truth in this, not inexplicable in the post eaten-apple world, that millions of people would desire to leave the gun and take the cannoli after plugging that *streutz* Paulie, who had it coming. But as Sharon Goldstein had resisted David, and as David had ignored God—who, come to think of it, hadn't tried nearly as hard with him as David had with Sharon—David sneered at the Orbachs' velvet-rope appeal to his celebrity vanity. Guilt may have been the new shame and 50 the new 30, but at the same time 29 was the new 39, and it was time for everyone to just fucking grow up and let a guy go home when he wants to. What, he wondered verbally to Mrs. Orbach, was he supposed to get out of being in Crazy Joey's posse? A profile in *Cosa Nostra Today?* The role of Maggio in *From Here to Eternity?* A treasure map of downtown Hoboken with X marking Jimmy Hoffa's sidewalk? It may have worked out okay for Yoko, said David, being in John's posse, but brother Michael's didn't do much for Fredo's career prospects. For that matter, God's hadn't exactly been a limo ride for that Christ kid. Besides, David uttered in conclusion, hanging with Crazy Joey was already too much like a full-season booking on *Fear Factor*.

And away did David take his leave, more exhausted now than Quasimodo at noon on Good Friday. Yea, though, his words must have been weighted with cunning suasion— either that or they had already party-pooped all the fun out of the whole rest of the night—for the Orbachs also chose to call it a night early, and accompanied not Crazy Joey to Umberto's Clam House. And this turned out to be a such a blessing, for whatever it was that Crazy ordered off the menu that late night in celebration of his birthday, what he quickly came to eat as a last meal was some sidewalk after a Pellicano appetizer and a main dish of Rigatoni Soprano.

This good fortune therefore gave Mr. Orbach appropriate availability among the living to star for the coming eons in many adored entertainments, including four thousand episodes of *Law and Order*. So it was a mitzvah for all—and proved to David, if not also God, who had to make the final call on this one, that there may be value in all things under heaven, including laziness and disrespect.*

---

* I read about the hit on Crazy Joey Gallo when I woke the next morning and saw the *Times*. I immediately chastised myself for my pathetic need to rush home and park on the couch in front of some dull television show. *Oh, if only I'd accompanied the Gallos to Umberto's Clam House*. It wasn't that I thought I could have saved my pal Joey from the assassins' bullets. It was that my career, dammit, would have really taken off.

39

And so it came to pass as the wind of the wolf passes at inopportune moments, like when you're alone in the elevator and suddenly it stops and someone really cute gets on, that a journal of news published each seven days titled cleverly *Newsweek* had chosen David for its whole Shroud of Turin treatment. And this was intended to be a big deal, with a photo on its cover, which even the Almighty Himself considered the ne plus ultra of having arrived full frontal in the Zeitgeist.

David, it seems, had proved himself brave and resourceful and relentless with his amusing material directed with glee at President Cruella de Nixon. And yea, unlike many weeks in prior annals when this journal's machers had selected for their big shout-out cover the image of a development that had by then passed onto the death slope of the Bell Curve of happeningness (see: *Ishtar*), this time they at the journal having the power to choose had correctly divined that comedy was the new rock 'n' roll (God's Plan in action, and working beautifully at that). And double lo and kudos to they for choosing to gift with a profile and avatar's cover image a genuine representative of such new comedy, rather than Señor Wences. And the man of the comedy they chose was David Steinberg.

For days that became weeks did the *Newsweek* man tag along with David as intelligence questions dog George Bush. O, the weeks extended themselves, too, with the man charged to write the story remaining present at each moment of David's life ("Pass the toilet paper, please"), observing, noting, following, recording, watching, chasing, perceiving, studying, intruding, examining, investigating, annoying, checking, and getting faced with David; and at last, when David pleaded that he was as void of further information as he was of interest in watching *Knot's Landing* did the writer complete his story. And only then did men with cameras arrive to capture a single perfect moment in which his eyes expressed laughter and his face declared "Buy this magazine"; and that took two weeks to get right. And thus was set the date for the story's appearance in the physical world. And that date was a Monday in early August. And David communicated with his mother, even, that he was to be so honored, and she asked whether his cover photo would be the one hanging still in the Winnipeg post office. And though she preferred that he occupy the cover of *The Forward* instead, she claimed that if he was happy, she was happy, subject to the usual limitations. And David insisted that he was happy indeed, and that his representatives were happier still, for his fee would now rise in much the same way that Monica rose from her knees to the A-list. "David," they described, "you're hot, hot, hot."

But in their giddiness, no one had thought to check Nostradamus, which is a mistake even God does not make, especially when investing in commodities futures. For when came that Monday it was not David's hot *punim* on the cover of the newsweekly journal; it was the shoe-shaped visage of that fucking Nixon, whom David always suspected would find a way to get the last laugh on him. Yea, it was newsworthy in extremis that the corrupt man kept in mind by Lord Acton had just days before abdicated his throne before the populace could drag him in chains naked through the cobblestones of Washington N.W.*

---

* A *Newsweek* story on Lily Tomlin, Richard Pryor, and me was scheduled to appear on the cover of the issue dated August 19, 1974, which meant that it would hit the streets the previous Monday—the 12th. For four months, *Newsweek* reporter Art Cooper, who later became the respected editor of *GQ*, had followed me around, attending numerous performances and interviewing me endlessly. "David," he'd say, "you have no idea what this story is going to mean to your career." He even gave me an early mockup of the cover art, with the photo of Lily, Richie, and me. To this day, I'm convinced that Richard Nixon had gotten word of the story and, to get even with me—a name prominently on his enemies' list—timed his resignation on Friday, August 9.

This turned out to be a double whammy for me, since I would have otherwise considered Nixon's resignation on August 9 the best birthday present I'd ever gotten. But Nixon obviously wanted to ruin the little Jew's birthday and also his life. He knew that *Newsweek* would immediately have to reshuffle and put his ugly mug on the cover instead of mine. Which was exactly what happened. Of course, the situation could have been salvaged in my favor. A reasonable person might reasonably conclude that the big story about America's top three up-and-coming comedians who were changing the face of comedy forever could simply be held for a week or two—even a month,

Agreed, this development was not as good for David as it might have been, but it was not bad either. It was, though, terrible for David Frye, who immediately offered to cut his fee for David Frost, for whom this would be very good.

---

if necessary. But no, the editing geniuses decided to run the story in the back of the Nixon-resignation issue, where no one ever saw it. My mother, on whose wall the cover art had been hanging, quietly observed, "Tatela, maybe they had no intention of ever putting you on the cover." What did she think, that he'd gone to the trouble of mocking up a cover just to make her feel good?

40

As if a man did flee from a lion, and a bear met him;
or went into the house, and leaned his hand on
the wall, and a serpent bit him—would not this
man be in a crapload of trouble? And should he not at least
move his ass and every other part of him ASAP from that
neighborhood and also out of this house that ought to be
red-tagged, or maybe even torched by Vinnie the Zippo?
And shall not the feast days full of solemn assemblies, with
burnt offerings and meat offerings that are high in cholesterol and saturated fats, be avoided religiously? Yea, these
were the questions asked long before the David Dinkins
years by that sourpuss Amos in his eponymous chapter
of the ancient Holy Book—unrhetorical questions that
David Steinberg had long before stopped seeking answers
to with any organized methodology requiring the attain-
ment of faith or the exertion of effort. Nor did he with any
earnestness regard the peace offerings of fat beasts who

tried doing an end-around with stomach staples, which is a similarly recurring theme in the aforementioned Book (his copy of which David had made to lie in a Simi Valley storage locker).

And why? Because, cowabunga, life was an excellent adventure for David Steinberg. He lived well and he was glad and pleased, dressing not in Members Only jackets with the collar up, taking not the charge from Yao Ming, provoking not Russell Crowe to anger, and needing not vials of clean urine from willing Mormons, though he would, on occasion, show off his Hustle under mirrored balls to the rhythms of "Disco Duck."

He played and he worked, and he worked and he played, but of course he played more than he worked, for this was the whole reason that he had gone into show business in the first place, as Xaviera Hollander had chosen her career for its home-office privileges. O, but there had been moments in this line of work that had been for David as unwelcome as party pimples, and these were the despairs when applause and lucre and fame sucked in comparison to sleeping far from his children; verily, it is on the road that comedians are appreciated. And paid. And so one day David had chosen no longer to open for Robert Goulet or close for Hervé Villechaize, his new line of work being no less audacious than Moses's change from desert rat to chief executive. Hark, David had become a director—as in telling people what to do toward the achievement of maximum effect on camera.

At first God was not down with this substitution, for it goes without saying that He does not always appreciate His people's use of their free will, and in this particular

case David was, not surprisingly, failing to hold up his end
of the Plan for the performance of laughter inducements.
True, David had no direct knowledge of the Plan which
God had conceived and implemented without his input;
he had simply learned to accept and enjoy unwittingly the
pleasant benefits of success as if he were Jim Belushi. But
God had gotten tired of carrying him all these years, seeing
to it that David received always good notices and better
bookings even though the little slug sometimes mailed it in
when he was moping and homesick. What, He wondered
anthropomorphically, was the difference if He let David
go like Clarabelle and Pinky Lee (or even John Belushi)?
After all, this was His way of things and had been since
Adam begged him in vain not to foreclose on Eden. So
why, then, against His better judgment, did He feel a certain inexplicable attachment to David—like Pam Ander-
son sticking with that twit Tommy Lee?

Alas, He was nothing if not a flexible God (snort at
your own risk), and as long as David continued to accept
the frequent invitations of the host of hosts to appear late
at night on television, often in lieu of the host himself, He
would allow David this midlife change—though first He
would make the kid pay punishing dues by giving him for
his debut a feature starring Burt Reynolds. After that, They
would be even. And then David could direct or produce or
do any fucking thing he wanted. Except MSNBC.

41

~❦~

This change in labors for David had not been the end of an era or an epoch or an eon or even a time. No, that end came to pass when the host of hosts drifted into the Malibu sunset one evening after uttering the words, "I bid you a very heartfelt good night." And David was present for this uttering, as he had been present all that week of adieus, and when the memories of laughter had been remembered, there quickly came tears. For what's true is that some of His earthly creatures can be known a mere ten minutes and seem to the knower centuries too much. But in the thirty years of Carson, we hardly knew you, Johnny.

THE NEW
TESTAMENT

42

For long, God had been far from David's thoughts, and love had been far from David's heart. And this, to David, was accepted fact without emotion, as that Canaanite Adonibezek learned to readjust after Judah cut off his big toes and thumbs (God's idea).

Then one day did David meet Robyn, and it was good, for she recognized not him as a man of fame and believed that the many who approached their table to offer well wishes were previously acquainted. And this was as endearing and welcome and charming as she was, so there were a multitude of good reasons to meet further. (O, how excellent it was, too, that she looked like a shiksa but wasn't.) And soon David and Robyn knew each other, and then they did know each other well, and after that David exhumed love for his second time, which was lovelier now and made all of life a comedy again. And, because he is no dummy, he of course did ask her to become his betrothed, and she agreed yes with enjoyment.

Thus were plans made for a nuptial at which they would swear to break never their covenant with each other. It was to be a small and quiet ceremony in the office of a secular man duly empowered by the law to affix his words and signature to their troth, for they believed there was no reason to make of this a big *chazzerai* megillah; its importance was in the union itself, not the rite. But then did friends from the town of Little Mountain, all of which they owned, insist upon a mini megillah atop their little mountain. With caterers.

This meant that now they would have to invite a rabbi. And others. Though not so many others as some others might have liked. The list contained only two concentric circles, the inner circle and the one outside, which left some on the outside but kept the proceeding only to those who would have died not to be there rather than including those who would ask of their mates, "Oy, do we really have to go all the way up there?" And this was a mitzvah for all concerned.

Now came the appointed day in the month when rains often wash away the mountain, yet on this day did the sun shine its glad yellow light on the assembled. Now did the rabbi take his place and with honey words welcome those who had come to spectate and benedict.

And now did David, who knows a little something about entrances, make his way down the aisle, his feet born aloft by Stardust and music, his heart gladdened and moved by the occasion and also by each of the faces which he took time to meet with his eyes in full. Then at last did he assume his place under the chuppa as came his bride toward him.*

And in turning to her did he notice a new face, one unnoticed before. It was a face he recognized not and yet recognized wholly—the face of not one man but all men and at once no men; women, too. And David was heartened by this welcome presence of an uninvited Guest, and he smiled, reacquainted at last with this bygone Friend whom he had long ago forsaken.

And now, in those slow-motion moments before Robyn reached him and became his wife, did David offer quiet thanks for his wonderful life which had been rich with blessings. And was not even half over.

Knock wood.

---

* My wedding to the former Robyn Todd was held at the Montecito, California, home of Ross and Janice Bagdasarian, keepers of the Alvin and the Chipmunks' legacy. The music I chose to accompany me on my dance down the aisle was the Beatles' "When I'm Sixty-Four" ("Will you still need me/will you still feed me"), which got a big laugh from the small crowd. I had reluctantly rejected the Chipmunks' cover of the song as being a little over the top, but it remains my preferred version. Husband and wife, I'm pleased to say, are still laughing.